CONDUCTING NECESSARY CONDITION ANALYSIS

for BUSINESS *and* MANAGEMENT STUDENTS

JAN DUL

Sara Miller McCune founded SAGE Publishing in 1965 to support the dissemination of usable knowledge and educate a global community. SAGE publishes more than 1000 journals and over 800 new books each year, spanning a wide range of subject areas. Our growing selection of library products includes archives, data, case studies and video. SAGE remains majority owned by our founder and after her lifetime will become owned by a charitable trust that secures the company's continued independence.

Los Angeles | London | New Delhi | Singapore | Washington DC | Melbourne

CONDUCTING NECESSARY CONDITION ANALYSIS

for BUSINESS and MANAGEMENT STUDENTS

JAN DUL

Los Angeles | London | New Delhi
Singapore | Washington DC | Melbourne

Los Angeles | London | New Delhi
Singapore | Washington DC | Melbourne

SAGE Publications Ltd
1 Oliver's Yard
55 City Road
London EC1Y 1SP

SAGE Publications Inc.
2455 Teller Road
Thousand Oaks, California 91320

SAGE Publications India Pvt Ltd
B 1/I 1 Mohan Cooperative Industrial Area
Mathura Road
New Delhi 110 044

SAGE Publications Asia-Pacific Pte Ltd
3 Church Street
#10-04 Samsung Hub
Singapore 049483

Editor: Ruth Stitt
Assistant editor: Martha Cunneen
Production editor: Sarah Cooke
Marketing manager: Lucia Sweet
Cover design: Francis Kenney
Typeset by: C&M Digitals (P) Ltd, Chennai, India
Printed in the UK

Library of Congress Control Number: 2019932721

British Library Cataloguing in Publication data

A catalogue record for this book is available from
the British Library

ISBN 978-1-52646-013-4
ISBN 978-1-52646-014-1 (pbk)

At SAGE we take sustainability seriously. Most of our products are printed in the UK using responsibly sourced
papers and boards. When we print overseas we ensure sustainable papers are used as measured by the PREPS
grading system. We undertake an annual audit to monitor our sustainability.

CONTENTS

LIST OF FIGURES AND TABLES

FIGURES

TABLES

EDITORS' INTRODUCTION TO THE *MASTERING BUSINESS RESEARCH METHODS* SERIES

Welcome to the *Mastering Business Research Methods* series. In recent years, there has been a great increase in the numbers of students reading for Master's level degrees across the business and management disciplines. A considerable number of these students are expected to prepare a dissertation towards the end of their degree programme in a timeframe of three to four months. For many this takes place after their taught modules have finished and is expected to be an independent piece of work. While each student is supported in their dissertation or research project by an academic supervisor, they will need to find out more detailed information about the method that they intend to use. Before starting such a project, students have usually been provided with little more than an overview of a wide range of methods in preparation for what is often a daunting task. If you are one such student, you are not alone. As university professors with a deep interest in research methods, we have provided this series of books to help people like you. Each book gives detailed information about a particular method, approach or task to support you in your dissertation. We understand both what is involved in Master's level dissertations and what help students need to understand research methods in order to excel when writing a dissertation. This series is the only one that is designed with the specific objective of helping Master's level students to prepare their dissertations.

Most books in our series are dedicated to either a method of data collection or a method of data analysis. They are intended to be read by you when undertaking the particular stage of the research process – of either data collection or analysis – and they are designed to provide sufficient knowledge for you to complete that stage. There are some other books in the series, such as those on *Mixed Methods* or *Action Research*, where the nature of the approach means that one method is inextricably linked with others. Those books are designed to provide you with a comprehensive understanding of the approach, although it may be necessary to supplement your reading of one or other of these books by reading another book on a particular method that you intend to employ when utilising that approach. All books in the series are written in a clear way by highly respected authors who have considerable experience of teaching and writing about research methods. To help you find your way around each one, we have utilised a standard format. That is to say that each book is organised into six chapters:

- **Chapter 1** introduces the method, considers how the method emerged for what purposes, and provides an outline of the remainder of the book.
- **Chapter 2** addresses the underlying philosophical assumptions that inform the uses of particular methods.
- **Chapter 3** discusses the components of the relevant method.
- **Chapter 4** considers the way in which the different components may be organised to use the method.
- **Chapter 5** provides examples of published studies that have used the method.
- **Chapter 6** concludes by reflecting on the strengths and weaknesses of that method.

We hope that reading your chosen books helps you in your dissertation.

Bill Lee, Mark N.K. Saunders and V.K. Narayanan

ABOUT THE SERIES EDITORS

Bill Lee, PhD is Professor of Accounting at the University of Sheffield, UK. He has a long-standing interest in research methods and practice, in addition to his research into accounting and accountability issues. Bill's research has been published widely, including in: *Accounting Forum*; *British Accounting Review*; *Critical Perspectives on Accounting*; *Journal of Applied Behavioral Science*; *Management Accounting Research*; *Omega*; *Organization Studies*; and *Work, Employment & Society*. His publications in the area of research methods and practice include the co-edited collections *The Real Life Guide to Accounting Research* and *Challenges and Controversies in Management Research*.

Mark N.K. Saunders BA MSc PGCE PhD FCIPD is Professor of Business Research Methods and Director of PhD Programmes at Birmingham Business School, University of Birmingham, UK. His research interests are research methods, in particular methods for participant selection and for understanding intra-organisational relationships; human resource aspects of the management of change, in particular trust within and between organisations; and small- and medium-sized enterprises. Mark's research has been published in journals including: *British Journal of Management*; *Journal of Small Business Management*; *Field Methods*; *Human Relations*; *Management Learning*; and *R&D Management*, *Social Science and Medicine*. He has co-authored and co-edited a range of books including *Research Methods for Business Students* (currently in its seventh edition) and the *Handbook of Research Methods on Trust* (currently in its second edition).

V.K. Narayanan is the Deloitte Touché Stubbs Professor of Strategy and Entre-preneurship in Le Bow College of Business, Drexel University, Philadelphia, PA, USA. His research has appeared in leading professional journals such as: *Academy of Management Journal*; *Academy of Management Review*; *Accounting Organizations and Society*; *Journal of Applied Psychology*; *Journal of Management*; *Journal of Management Studies*; *Management Information Systems Quarterly*; *R&D Management*; and *Strategic Management Journal*. He has authored or co-authored several books, including *Managing Technology and Innovation for Competitive Advantage*, and has co-edited the *Encyclopaedia of Technology and Innovation Management*.

ABOUT THE AUTHOR

Jan Dul is a professor of Technology and Human Factors at Rotterdam School of Management, Erasmus University, the Netherlands. His research focuses on work environments for human performance and well-being. He is strongly interested in empirical research methodology. Jan has written more than 150 publications. His methodological publications include a book on case study methodology in business research co-authored with Tony Hak. He is the founder of Necessary Condition Analysis (NCA), and has published about it in methodological journals such as *Organizational Research Methods* and *Sociological Methods & Research*.

ACKNOWLEDGEMENTS

The thinking behind the book originated at least ten years ago and I am grateful to all who have contributed since then. In the beginning I had many discussions with Tony Hak about research methodology in general and necessity analysis in particular. While I was writing this book, Tony sadly passed away. Gary Goertz is another buddy from the beginning. I could discuss with him many complexities about necessity analysis and about integrating necessity thinking in contexts that are not common to it. Barbara Vis introduced me to the world of Qualitative Comparative Analysis (QCA) and we thoroughly discussed the differences between Necessary Condition Analysis (NCA) and QCA. Roelof Kuik, Erwin van der Laan and I accepted the challenge of developing statistical tests for NCA. Scientific programmer Govert Buijs was able to make sense of my original R script for NCA, and turned it into a professional package. It was a pleasure to help Maciej Karwowski, and Wendy van der Valk and Regien Sumo with writing their first NCA articles, which were the first published applications of NCA.

In recent years, I have worked intensively with the 'NCA Ambassadors' Zsófia Tóth, Sven Hauff and Stefan Breet, who have been among the earliest adopters of NCA and who helped to organise, and participate in, workshops and discussions about NCA all over the world. They also commented on earlier versions of this book, just as several other people did, including Jorick Alberga, Florence Allard-Poesi, Gary Goertz, Colleen Kordish, Erwin van der Laan, Henk van Rhee, and Pauline Thieule. Furthermore, I am grateful to Babis Saridakis, Dionysis Skarmeas and Constantinos Leonidou for providing their dataset on corporate social responsibility, and to Wilfred Knol, Jannes Slomp, Roel Schouteten and Kristina Lauche for providing their dataset on lean manufacturing. This allowed me to re-analyse of their data with NCA. I would also like to sincerely thank Monique van Donzel, Krista Schellevis and other staff from the Erasmus Research Institute of Management for their organisational and technical support over many years, including support for developing and maintaining the NCA website. Finally, I would like to thank my colleagues Steef van de Velde, Marno Verbeek, Pursey Heugens, Eric van Heck, René de Koster and Finn Wynstra for giving me the opportunity and support necessary for developing NCA and writing this book.

1

INTRODUCTION

ABOUT THIS BOOK

Necessary conditions are everywhere. Travelling to Amsterdam is a necessary condition for seeing Rembrandt's painting *The Night Watch* in person. If you want to drive a car you will need fuel, if you want to graduate you will need to write a dissertation or satisfy the conditions of your programme, and if you want to read this book you will need to open it. Opening the book is a necessary condition because it enables you to read it. This is a very strong condition because not opening the book guarantees that you will not read it. However, opening the book is not a sufficient condition for reading it. After opening it you may decide not to read it; other factors such as motivation and time may play a role as well. Thus, a *necessary but not sufficient condition* enables the presence of the outcome when present, guarantees the absence of the outcome when absent, but does not guarantee the presence of the outcome when present. Absence of the necessary condition is a bottleneck that perfectly predicts the absence of the outcome. If you do not open the book, you will not read it.

Thank you for opening the book! You may find the motivation and time to read it in its entirety such that you can familiarise yourself with Necessary Condition Analysis (NCA). NCA is a research approach and data analysis method that is based on the logic that factors can be necessary but not sufficient for an outcome to occur. Because necessary conditions are everywhere in real life, NCA can be used in any discipline and profession. In psychology it has been found that intelligence is necessary but not sufficient for creativity: if persons are not intelligent they are not creative, but if they are intelligent they may or may not be creative (Karwowski et al., 2016). In business it is discussed whether senior management commitment is necessary but not sufficient for successful organisational change: if there is no senior management commitment then change will not be successful, but if there is senior management commitment then change may or may not be successful (Knol et al., 2018). In medicine it has been found that meta-cognition – the capacity to identify and then integrate mental experiences – is necessary for motivation of people with schizophrenia for good functioning: if there is not enough meta-cognition then motivation is low, but if meta-cognition is high, motivation may be low or high (Luther et al., 2017).

WHY IS NCA VALUABLE?

NCA is valuable for several reasons. First, the method is intuitive and straightforward. Any researcher with a basic knowledge of scientific research and research methodology can readily apply the method. Second, the method triggers a new way of theoretical thinking that is based on necessity logic. Therefore, a study with NCA can provide an interesting theoretical contribution. Third, because the necessary condition works in isolation from the rest of the causal structure (that is why it is necessary), the theoretical necessity model can be simple. Often, NCA researchers will employ a theoretical model with only one or a few potential necessity causes. Fourth, the method complements other methodologies that are not based on necessity logic, such as regression analysis. Fifth, the results of NCA can be immediately applied in practice. If a necessary condition is identified, that condition must be in place in virtually every single case to reach the outcome. If that condition is not in place, the outcome will not occur. Thus, it makes sense only to focus on this condition before focusing on other causes to influence the outcome. Practitioners use this necessity logic when designing, managing or controlling factors to influence an outcome. They are aware that in a complex (social) environment it is not possible to design, manage and control all factors, so they focus on crucial factors that must be present to avoid a guaranteed failure, in other words the necessary conditions. Researchers who attended a summer course on NCA have provided their thoughts on why NCA could be useful (Box 1.1).

Box 1.1   Opinions of NCA users about NCA

Intuitive and straightforward:	*Triggers new theoretical insights:*
'Intuitively easy to understand'	'Shifts the focus to the most important drivers of an outcome --> from nice-to-have to need-to-have'
'Easy to implement'	
'Easy to understand/logical'	'It's a new way of thinking and therefore it may lead to many interesting insights, just reanalysing old datasets'

'User-friendliness: easy to learn: all analyses can be done within 15 minutes; visualisation of outcomes is easy'

'Simple technique that requires no 'preparation', data transformation, manipulation, and correction. A perfect plug-and-play method that can give output in under 10 minutes'

'It allows you to test a theory using a small set of observations'

'I do believe that is has great exploratory value that is congruent with the recent emphasis on big data'

'Get on the NCA wave; doors will open when successful'

High relevance for practice:

'If there is a necessary condition its implications to practice are clear-cut and strong'

'Insights are very relevant for practice'

'Practically relevant!'

'Very relevant for practice'

'Opportunity to make truly novel/strong theoretical contributions'

'Could have potential breakthrough insights in the way we view causality and also reverse causality'

'This method can advance our understanding by providing a new perspective on causal relationship'

Complements other methods:

'Analysis provides insights that cannot be obtained with another method'

'Provides a radically different perspective on existing data'

'Ability to test theoretical assumptions that are currently often overlooked or taken for granted in a rigorous way'

'Different approach to analysis for a completely different, yet very relevant question'

HOW TO CONDUCT NCA?

NCA can be conducted in four stages (Figure 1.1).

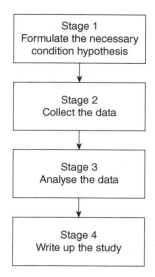

Figure 1.1   The four stages of conducting Necessary Condition Analysis

In *Stage 1* the researcher formulates the necessary condition hypothesis: 'X is necessary for Y'. It is possible to formulate more than one hypothesis. In *Stage 2* the researcher collects the data that are needed to perform NCA. This stage includes the selecting or sampling of cases, and the measurement of X and Y for each case, resulting in a dataset. It is also possible to use an existing dataset. *Stage 3* is the core of NCA where the dataset is analysed regarding necessity and a conclusion is drawn about the necessary condition hypothesis. In *Stage 4* the researcher reports the results of the NCA study.

WHERE IS NCA APPLIED?

NCA can be valuable to researchers who want to conduct a new research project that is based on necessity logic or extend an existing research project to add novelty and offer additional insights. NCA can provide results that are academically rigorous and practically relevant. Such a project could be a PhD thesis, or a study for publication in a journal, or most meaningfully for this book, a Master's dissertation. Since the availability of NCA's core article in 2016 (Dul, 2016a) and the related free NCA software (Dul and Buijs, 2015), the method has been applied in many disciplines, including a variety of business and management fields. Examples include Strategy, Finance, Operations, Innovation, Information Management, Human Resource Management, Organisational Behaviour, Entrepreneurship, and Transportation (Box 1.2). Business and management students have also used NCA for their Master's theses with success (Box 1.3).

Box 1.2   Examples of NCA applications in business and management

- Corporate Social Performance: a Necessary Condition Analysis (Van der Laan and Dul, 2016).
- Is Brokerage Necessary for Innovative Performance? A Necessary Condition Analysis (Breet et al., 2018).
- Firm Capabilities and Performance: a Necessary Condition Analysis (Tho, 2018).
- Success and Failure of Nascent Stock Markets (Albuquerque de Sousa et al., 2016).
- Implementing Lean Practices in Manufacturing SMEs: Testing critical success factors using Necessary Condition Analysis (Knol et al., 2018).
- A Methodological Demonstration of Set-theoretical Approach to Social Media Maturity Models using Necessary Condition Analysis (Lasrado et al., 2016).
- When are Contracts and Trust Necessary for Innovation in Buyer-supplier Relationships? A Necessary Condition Analysis (Van der Valk et al., 2016).

- Is High Performance Without High Performance Work Practices Possible? A Necessary Condition Analysis (Hauff et al., 2017).
- Is Creativity Without Intelligence Possible? A Necessary Condition Analysis (Karwowski et al., 2016).
- No Particular Action Needed? A Necessary Condition Analysis of gestation activities and firm emergence (Arenius et al., 2017).
- Determinants of Safe and Productive Truck Driving: Empirical evidence from long-haul cargo transport (De Vries et al., 2017).

Box 1.3 Examples of Master's theses with NCA applications in business and management

- Necessary Conditions for Maintaining Physical Activity Interventions (Guiking, 2009).
- Critical success factors of firms that cooperate in innovation (Sarrucco, 2011).
- Necessary conditional hypotheses building and occupational safety in Dutch warehouses (Bakker, 2011).
- Critical success factors for IT project success (Verheul, 2013).
- Explaining employee satisfaction with the headquarter-subsidiary relationship (Van Dalen, 2014).
- Critical success factors of new product development in the medical industry (Meijer, 2014).
- Critical success factors for information system success within the empty container positioning process (Helwig, 2014).
- Customer orientation and business performance: a content analysis of Dutch SMEs' websites (Van 't Hul, 2015).
- The effect of capital structure and corporate governance on stock liquidity (Kuipers, 2016).
- Necessary conditions for new ventures' positive performances (Ferrari, 2016).
- Software-based platform ecosystems: relationship between vertical openness and performance (Overschie, 2016).
- Testing the necessary conditions of technology acceptance by potential organisational users of a mandatory IT in the pre-implementation phase (Verhoeve, 2017).
- The necessary conditions for entrepreneurial behaviour by middle management (Smits, 2018).
- The role of organisational factors in the pursuit of exploratory innovation across business units: a Necessary Condition Analysis (Thieule, 2018).

NCA has been applied to many types of research questions, both in qualitative research and in quantitative research. In qualitative research usually a small number of cases are studied, normally less than 20. I call this a 'small N study', where N stands for the number of cases. Most of the studies until 2016 that are presented in Box 1.3 are examples of small N studies. In quantitative research a large number of cases are studied with usually more than 20 cases. This is called a 'large N study'. All the studies in Box 1.2 are examples of large N studies. The study with the largest N is a study with 12,255 persons showing that intelligence is necessary for creativity (Karwowski et al., 2016). In both qualitative and quantitative research, the research question often deals with characteristics, efforts, or steps that can be managed, designed or controlled for reaching or preventing an outcome that is of interest. That outcome can be something desirable, e.g. performance, innovation, sustainability, financial results, change, creativity, well-being, or health. In the selected business and management studies of Box 1.2 and Box 1.3 most of the outcomes are business outcomes like financial performance, innovation performance or social performance. When the desirable outcome is formulated as 'success', the necessary condition is sometimes called a 'critical success factor', or 'key success factor', as several examples in Box 1.3 show. Hence, 'critical' means that the factor must be present for success and that there will be a guaranteed failure if the factor is absent. The outcome can also be something undesirable, e.g. stress, sickness, risk, disease, or failure. Thus, the absence of the necessary condition ensures the absence of the undesired outcome. Without the tubercle bacteria a person does not have tuberculosis.

Gary Goertz, one of the modern thinkers about necessity logic and research, states that 'for any research area one can find important necessary condition hypotheses' (Goertz and Starr, 2003: 65-66). I support this statement wholeheartedly for any social science area including business and management. My discussions with researchers and students in all kinds of research areas show that it is always possible to quickly formulate that X, which is something that can be influenced in practice, such as enough funding for a change project, is necessary for Y, which is some outcome that is of interest in practice, such as successful change. Most likely, necessity logic also applies to your topic of research, and you could formulate a research question that can be answered with NCA. In Appendix 1, I give recommendations for how research questions and necessary condition hypotheses can be formulated for any research topic.

A BRIEF HISTORY OF NCA

Although NCA is a new research methodology, its logic goes back to David Hume's philosophy of science (1777), and even to Aristotle (350 BC). Necessity *statements* are common in any research discipline and practice. However, necessary condition *analysis* in terms of developing or testing necessity statements with data has been absent for a long time. The simple reason is that no such analysis method was available. Since Francis Galton's (1886) discovery of correlation and regression, the research focus has been on regression analysis and its underlying additive average effect logic: predicting the outcome (on average) from one or several predictors. Such analyses, however, cannot assess the necessity of single predictors.

Recently, the methodological interest in necessity analysis was revived. In 1987, Charles Ragin introduced a methodology called Qualitative Comparative Analysis (QCA) that includes the analysis of binary necessity statements, in effect 'presence/absence of X is necessary for presence/absence of Y'. However, in the years that followed QCA primarily focused on sufficiency analysis, i.e. identifying alternative combinations of conditions that are sufficient for the outcome. Currently, QCA's necessity analysis is usually recommended to precede the sufficiency analysis, but QCA applications in business and management in particular regularly lack a necessity analysis. This can be observed, for example, in the *Journal of Business Research* that has published a large number of QCA studies in business and management. For a discussion on the differences between NCA and QCA see Dul (2016b) and Vis and Dul (2018).

Around the turn of the century, several researchers in political science stressed the importance of necessary conditions in their field of research (Dion, 1998; Braumoeller and Goertz, 2000; Ragin, 2000). In 2003, building on these developments, Gary Goertz and Harvey Starr published *Necessary Conditions: Theory, Methodology, and Applications*, in which they discussed and integrated a broad range of topics related to necessity logic (Goertz and Starr, 2003). Their book identifies potential directions for the methodological development of necessity analysis and its potential application in political science and sociology. Later, in 2008, Tony Hak and I integrated necessity analysis in our book *Case Study Methodology in Business Research* (Dul and Hak, 2008). We suggested using necessity logic and analysis in business and management research, and showed how it can be applied not only in small N case studies but also in large N studies. Afterwards we combined forces and developed necessity analysis beyond binary necessity analysis (Dul, et al. 2010; Goertz, Hak, and Dul, 2013). Our goal was to perform a necessity analysis not just with variables that have only two levels (e.g. absent/present), the necessary conditions *in kind*, but also with variables that have more than two levels. This allows us to make a more precise *in degree* necessity statement in terms of 'level of X is necessary for level of Y'. For example, 20 minutes of reading time are necessary for finishing Chapter 1 of this book and several hours of reading time are necessary for finishing the entire book. From that period onwards, I focused my methodological research on necessity analysis and on developing an integrated approach (including software) that can be used by qualitative and quantitative researchers who are interested in necessity logic. The first version of this integrated approach was published in 2016 in the journal *Organizational Research*

Methods (Dul, 2016a). In this book I build on this publication and include recent extensions and insights from discussions about NCA worldwide, and applications of NCA in many research areas.

NCA COMPARED TO OTHER MODELS AND METHODS

It is clear that NCA differs fundamentally from conventional theoretical models and data analysis methods like multiple regression and structural equation modelling. These models and methods focus on the *average effect* of a factor on the outcome. For example, on average Master's students and not Bachelor's students read this book. 'Study level' has an average effect on reading the book, but the factor is not necessary because Bachelor's students also read this book. It is possible that a factor not only has an average effect on the outcome, but is also necessary. For example, intelligence has an average effect on creativity because on average people who are more intelligent are also more creative. Intelligence is also necessary for creativity because it is practically impossible to find people with a high level of creativity without out a high level of intelligence.

Another main difference between NCA and conventional models and methods is that NCA focuses on the absence rather than the presence of a desired (e.g, health) or undesired (e.g. sickness) outcome. This has an important consequence for the complexity of the model. Most average effect models that explain on the presence of the outcome include many potential predictors and these models require 'control variables' to avoid biased estimations. Introducing more variables and complexity can result in better predictions of average effects of variables on the outcome. With the availability of better data analysis methods and faster computers, the current trend is to analyse more complex models. One unique feature of NCA is that it predicts the absence of the outcome. The absence of the outcome can be almost perfectly predicted by the absence of a single necessary condition. Thus, NCA can make valid predictions even with simple theoretical models.

The advantages of a simple model should not be underestimated. First, a simple model is parsimonious according to 'Occam's razor' principle. Parsimony avoids theories becoming too complex and incomprehensible. Parsimonious models are easier to understand and can generalise more reliably than complex models. More complexity does not necessary mean more predictive accuracy and insight, and additional variables may have diminishing returns. In one of the first published studies that applied NCA (Van der Valk et al., 2016), the theoretical model included only three necessary conditions and one outcome. This study on buyer-supplier relations included competence trust, goodwill trust, and contract detail as conditions, and innovation performance as outcome. It was found that each condition was necessary for innovative performance. Thus, the conditions could not compensate for each other. Second, with a simple model it is possible that all included variables have already been measured before in another study such that it may be possible to find an existing dataset that includes these variables. For example, datasets may have been built for obtaining insights on average effects with regression analysis, and when NCA is used with the same data new insights might be obtained. There is a plethora of currently available data that have not been analysed with NCA and that could be analysed for a greater depth of under-standing. Thus, an NCA study may be an 'archival data' or 'secondary data' study. Many datasets are publicly available in repositories, are available as supplementary material of published studies, or may be provided by individual researchers who are willing to share their data in the spirit of open science. In another early NCA application, Karwowski et al. (2016) used only existing datasets that had been pre-viously used for average effect analyses with regression analyses. They showed that intelligence is necessary for creativity and used a simple model with only one condition and one outcome. Although most NCA studies have used simple models, NCA can also handle complex models. For example, Nikita Bakker (2011), one of my Master's thesis students, evaluated 84(!) potential necessary conditions for safety in warehouses.

Thus, conventional methods search for an average effect, usually with a com-plex model, and NCA searches for necessary but not sufficient conditions, usually with a simple model. Both approaches are complementary; they are not competing. Therefore, it is possible to combine NCA with other methodologies to gain comple-mentary insights. For example, when NCA is combined with regression analysis, the insights about the necessity of the variable for the outcome can be combined with the insights about the average contribution of the variable (e.g. De Vries et al., 2017). It is also possible to combine NCA with QCA. QCA focuses on sufficiency, hence on how the outcome can be produced by multiple possible combinations of conditions. QCA also has an 'in kind' necessity approach. A QCA analysis can be enriched with the insights from NCA's 'in degree' necessity approach about which level of the condition must be in place in all sufficient combinations to ensure that these combinations can indeed produce the outcome (e.g. Fredrich et al., 2019). When NCA is combined with other methods, the study includes a usually more complex theoretical model in Stage 1, and a more extensive data analysis in Stage 3. Most of the examples in Box 1.2 and Box 1.3 use NCA as the only or main logic and methodology. For these it is straight-forward to write a consistent story based on necessity logic.

THE REMAINDER OF THIS BOOK

In the remainder of this book I will guide you through the process of conduct-ing research with NCA. In Chapters 2 and 3 I will explain more about the logic and backgrounds of NCA. These sections are important for your understanding of necessity logic and its theoretical statements and of the underlying principles of NCA. This knowledge is not only important for your own knowledge, but also for being able to respond properly to comments from researchers such as from colleagues, supervisors, or reviewers who may lack familiarity with NCA. Chapter 4 describes *how* to conduct NCA's data analysis. I distinguish between the application of NCA with the 'contingency table approach' that includes a *qualitative* visual inspection of the data, and the application of NCA with the 'scatter plot approach' that includes a *quantitative* data analysis with the NCA software. In Chapter 5, I illustrate how researchers have used NCA. Any researcher faces methodological dilemmas when conducting research. I will review how the researchers have applied NCA and handled dilemmas. The book concludes with Chapter 6 which covers the strengths and weaknesses of NCA.

You have managed to keep the book open and have spent some 20 minutes reading it. I hope that you continue reading it. While doing so you may come up with some questions that are not addressed in the book. You may then wish to consult the NCA website (www.erim.nl/nca), which contains a wealth of information about NCA. It has a special section about this book, where you can find supplementary materials, such as how to combine NCA with regression analysis or how to combine NCA with QCA. The R scripts that are used for certain figures and analyses in this book can also be found there. Furthermore, you can leave comments about the book, such that I can improve it when it is updated. You can also become a member of the NCA community to discuss the method and its applications, ask help from other NCA researchers, and - after a while - possibly advise other researchers on how to conduct NCA. You may soon become one of the first NCA experts in your field!

2

PHILOSOPHICAL ASSUMPTIONS
AND LOGIC OF NCA

INTRODUCTION

In this chapter I will discuss backgrounds of NCA in terms of the philosophical assumptions that underlie research with NCA and the fundamentals of its necessity logic. I will show that necessary conditions can be formulated in different ways and I will extend binary necessity logic, i.e. logic with dichotomous variables that can have only two levels, to necessity logic with discrete variables that can have a finite number of levels, and necessity logic with continuous variables that can have an infinite number of levels. Finally, I will show that necessity logic is all around us in practice and research.

PHILOSOPHICAL ASSUMPTIONS

NCA is compatible with various philosophical assumptions about reality (ontology) and about approaches to knowledge creation (epistemology). Ontological positions range from realism that sees the social world as having a reality independent of an individual, through positions that view different dimensions of the social world as having different degrees of independence, to positions that view the social world as having no independence and being a construction of the interactions of participants in that world. Epistemological positions range from positivism that assumes an objective and universal applicability of scientific researchers' observations of reality, through positions that believe observations and meanings are context-bound and specific to communities, to positions that emphasise the subjectivity in all human interpretations and suggest that researchers should focus on these interpretations.

Positivism – which assumes a realist ontology – is the mainstream framework in the natural sciences and most of the social sciences including most of business and management research. Not surprisingly, most NCA research until now has been based on the positivist framework. An NCA study that is based on the positivist framework assumes that there is a reality 'out there'. Positivists formulate a necessity theoretical assumption about this reality – the necessary condition hypothesis – and test it with empirical data. They prefer an objective approach to analyse the data and to test by falsification whether the data support the hypothesis. Positivists attempt to generalise the results beyond the cases that were studied.

NCA's logic could also be used with an interpretivist framework. An NCA study that is based on the interpretivist framework would assume that people make sense of reality through a necessity logic. Such research investigates how people perceive reality. The researcher is engaged in the subject, reflects on the perceptions of people and on their own observations, and describes the findings in a transparent 'thick' description. Usually no attempts are made to generalise from the studied case with its specific context to a wider set of cases. Both the positivist and the interpretivist frameworks can use quantitative and qualitative data and respective data analyses methods, although quantitative data and data analysis are dominant in the positivist approach and qualitative data and data analysis are dominant in the interpretivist approach.

In this book I focus on NCA within the positivist framework. I assume that:

- the researcher tries to capture reality;
- selected or sampled cases represent this reality;
- measurement is undertaken to quantify or qualify the properties of these cases;
- hypotheses are empirically tested by using falsification;
- the study attempts to make analytical or statistical generalisations beyond the studied cases.

I will show – within this positivist framework – how NCA is broadly applicable. NCA can be used with qualitative data using words or letters or with quantitative data using numbers. NCA can be used with qualitative data analysis by visual inspection, or with quantitative data analysis by using mathematics and statistics. NCA can be used with single case studies where N = 1, multiple case studies where N = small, or 'big data' studies where N = large. N is the number of cases that are studied.

NECESSITY LOGIC

One fundamental goal of scientific research is to identify the causal relationships between concepts of interest. When the relationship between concept X that causes concept Y is known, it is possible to make predictions about how Y changes by the changes in X. X is usually called 'cause', 'independent variable', 'factor', 'determinant', 'predictor' or 'condition', and Y is called 'effect', 'dependent variable' or 'outcome'. NCA prefers the terms 'condition' and 'outcome'. The most common interpretation of 'X causes Y' is that X 'produces' Y. A change in X results in a change in Y. This is 'sufficiency' causal logic, i.e. a change in X is sufficient for a change in Y.

Hume (1711-1776) described causality as follows:

> We may define a cause to be an object, followed by another, and where all the objects, similar to the first, are followed by objects, similar to the second. Or in other words, where, if the first had not been, the second never had existed. (Hume, 1777)

In the first sentence Hume refers to sufficiency logic: objects X are followed by objects Y. In the second sentence he states that without X there is no Y. This refers to necessity logic. The absence of X guarantees the absence of Y. Hence, one may say that Hume introduced two types of causes: sufficient causes that produce the outcome when present, and necessary causes that guarantee the absence of the outcome when absent.

Necessary and sufficient causes

Given the distinction between necessary and sufficient causes, X can have three types of causal effect on Y:

- *X is sufficient, but not necessary for Y.* When it rains (X), the ground gets wet (Y). Rain is a sufficient condition for wet ground. However other causes, e.g. flooding, can make the ground wet. Thus, rain is not necessary for wet ground.
- *X is necessary, but not sufficient for Y.* A car must have fuel (X) to move (Y). Fuel is necessary for a moving car. However, a car with fuel may also stand still. Thus, fuel is not sufficient for a moving car.
- *X is sufficient and necessary for Y.* Having passed the voting age (X) is necessary and sufficient for having the right to vote (Y).

Notice that causal statements do not need to be universally true. They usually hold within a certain domain of application. With an umbrella, rain may not make the ground wet. The causal statement that rain is sufficient for wet ground holds only when there are no obstacles. A car may move down a hill without fuel. The causal statement that fuel is necessary for moving holds when the car is driven in a flat area; the truth of the statement also depends on how you define 'fuel' (e.g. including petrol and electricity). In certain countries woman may not have voting rights. Thus, the causal statement that voting age is necessary and sufficient for voting right holds for countries with universal suffrage. For the above examples you can probably find more exceptions. Exploring the borders of a causal statement by searching for exceptions is an important aspect of the process of specifying where the causal statement is supposed to hold, hence defining the *theoretical domain* of the hypothesis. Only within this domain is the causal statement claimed to be true, and it may be that new exceptions will lead to redefining the theoretical domain. This is true for any theory development process.

The three types of causes are illustrated in Figure 2.1. This figure shows three XY tables, or 'contingency tables', where X is the cause on the horizontal axis and Y is the effect on the vertical axis. X and Y are dichotomous (binary) concepts that can have only two values, e.g. absent or present, 0 and 1, or low and high, etc.

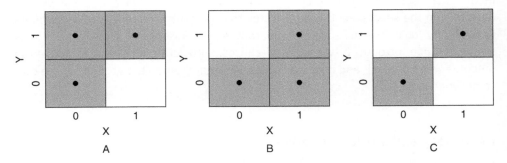

Figure 2.1 Illustration of three types of causes with dichotomous concepts.
A: X is sufficient but not necessary for Y. B: X is necessary but not sufficient for Y. C: X is necessary and sufficient for Y.

Each cell of a table represents a given combination of X and Y: the lower left cell represents the combination X = 0, Y = 0; the lower right cell represents the combination X = 1, Y = 0; the upper left cell represents the combination X = 0, Y = 1; and the upper right cell represents the combination X = 1, Y = 1. If a cell has a dot, this means that observations (cases) can exist for that particular combination of X and Y, when the specific statement applies. The absence of a dot means that no observation can exist for that particular combination of X and Y, when the specific statement applies. Figure 2.1A shows the possible combinations of values of X and Y when X is a *sufficient but not necessary* cause for Y. When X is present (value 1) Y is also present: X produces Y. However, when X is absent (value 0) Y can be absent or present. Figure 2.1B shows the possible combinations of values of X and Y when

X is a *necessary but not sufficient* cause for Y. When X is absent (value 0) Y is also absent. Absence of X produces absence of Y. However, when X is present (value 1) Y can be absent or present. Figure 2.1C shows the possible combinations of values of X and Y when X is a *necessary and sufficient* cause for Y. When X is present (value 1) Y is also present, and when X is absent Y is also absent. The presence of X produces the presence of Y, and the absence of Y produces the absence of Y.

Alternative formulations of necessary causes

The necessary cause can be formulated in two ways:

The presence of X is necessary for the presence of Y. This is the 'necessity of presence' or 'enabling' formulation of the necessary condition.

The absence of X is sufficient for the absence of Y. This is the 'sufficiency of absence' or 'constraining' formulation of the necessary condition.

Thus, when opening the book is a necessary cause for reading it, the necessity can be expressed in two ways:

Opening the book is necessary for reading the book.

Not opening the book is sufficient for not reading the book.

Both formulations are logically equivalent. In the 'necessity of presence' formulation the presence of the necessary cause enables the presence of the outcome. This formulation expresses the enabling role of the necessary condition. In the 'sufficiency of absence' formulation the absence of the necessary cause produces the absence of the outcome. This formulation expresses the constraining role of the necessary condition.

Other words are also used to refer to necessity logic. In Box 2.1 I distinguish between necessary conditions formulations in terms of enabling factors by using the necessity of the presence formulation, and necessary conditions formulations in terms of constraining factors by using the sufficiency of the absence formulation.

Many words that represent necessity logic are commonplace. Users may be unaware of their underlying logical meaning. The words are sometime confused with the 'importance' of a factor. However, an 'important' sufficient factor that contributes to the outcome may not be a necessary factor for the outcome, and a 'not important' factor may be necessary. A good starting point for identifying potential necessary conditions in a certain field is searching in the literature for words like those in Box 2.1, or identifying these words when researchers or practitioners talk about causal relations in their fields of expertise.

Box 2.1   Common words representing necessity logic (enablers and constraints)

Enablers (the presence of X is necessary for the presence of Y):

- X is necessary for Y
- X enables Y
- X is needed for Y
- X is critical for Y
- X is crucial for Y
- X is essential for Y
- X is indispensable for Y
- X is a prerequisite for Y
- X is a requirement for Y
- X is a conditio sine qua non for Y
- X is a precondition for Y
- X allows Y
- There must be X to have Y
- Y requires X

Constraints (the absence of X is sufficient for the absence of Y):

- X constrains Y
- X limits Y
- X blocks Y
- X bounds Y
- X stops Y
- X restricts Y
- X is a barrier for Y
- X is a bottleneck for Y
- Without X there cannot be Y
- Absence of X is sufficient for absence of Y

Empty spaces

In this book I follow the convention that cause X is shown on the horizontal axis of an XY table or plot with increasing values to the right. The outcome Y is shown on the vertical axis with higher values upwards. Consequently, when the presence of X is necessary for the presence of Y, the empty space where cases are not possible is in the upper left corner (as in Figure 2.1B). However, the empty space can also show up in another corner depending when the *absence of X* is the necessary condition, or when the *absence of Y* is the outcome. Figure 2.2 shows that an empty space in any corner can be formulated in terms of necessity, depending on whether X and Y are absent or present:

- Figure 2.2A – The *presence* of X is necessary for the *presence* of Y. The upper left corner is empty. The level Y = 1 (presence of Y) can only be achieved when X = 1 (presence of X). This is the most common understanding of the statement that 'X is necessary (but not sufficient) for Y'. Figure 2.2A corresponds to Figure 2.1B.
- Figure 2.2B – The *absence* of X is necessary (but not sufficient) for the *presence* of Y. The upper right corner is empty. In this situation the level Y = 1 (presence of Y) can only be achieved when X = 0 (absence of X). For example, when X is smoking and Y is long-term health, the necessity statement that non-smoking is necessary for long-term health (although not everybody may agree) results in an empty space in the upper right corner.

- Figure 2.2C – The *presence* of X is necessary (but not sufficient) for the *absence* of Y. Lower left corner is empty. This situation is somewhat less intuitive. The level Y = 0 (absence of Y) can only be achieved when X = 1 (presence of X). This corresponds to the statement that the absence of X is sufficient for the presence of Y. For example, when X is social support and Y is stress, the necessity statement that social support is necessary for no stress results in an empty space in the lower left corner.
- Figure 2.2D – The *absence* of X is necessary (but not sufficient) for the *absence* of Y. The lower right corner is empty. In this situation the level Y = 0 (absence of Y) can only be achieved when X = 0 (absence of X). For example, when X is Rain and Y is Wet ground, the necessity statement that the absence of Rain is a necessary for the absence of Wet ground (all dry ground had no rain) results in an empty space in the lower right corner. This corresponds to the statement that the presence of X is sufficient (but not necessary) for the presence of Y, which is the common sufficiency statement: Rain is sufficient for Wet ground. Therefore, Figure 2.2D corresponds to Figure 2.1A.

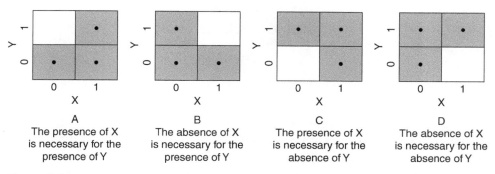

Figure 2.2   Four representations of 'X is necessary for Y' depending on the presence or absence of X and Y

By redefining X and Y (e.g. X = non-smoking instead of smoking; Y = no-stress instead of stress), the empty spaces will show up again in the upper left corner: the presence of non-smoking is necessary for the presence of health, and the presence of social support is necessary for the presence of no stress. In this book, unless otherwise stated, I define X and Y such that the necessity of X for Y corresponds to 'the presence of X is necessary for the presence of Y', and the empty space is in the upper left corner.

Deterministic and probabilistic views on necessity

What does it mean if the empty space is not entirely empty, hence that only a few cases are in the upper left corner that is otherwise empty? Is this reason enough to reject the necessity? In other words, does necessity require a deterministic view without exceptions? Or is it also possible to have a probabilistic view on necessity such as stating that X is 'practically', 'virtually', or 'almost always' necessary for Y? There are no simple answers to these questions. In the deterministic view on necessity any case in the empty space would falsify a necessity claim. For example, when one out of five cases is in the otherwise empty space it seems realistic to conclude that X is not necessary for Y. But if one case from 100 observed cases shows up in the 'empty space' the conclusion is less clear. Should we conclude that X is not necessary for Y, or should we conclude that X is 'almost always' necessary for Y? This situation occurs in Figure 2.3.

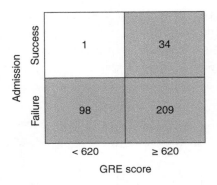

Figure 2.3   GRE scores and Admission to a graduate programme (after Vaisey, 2009)

In this example, 342 students applied for admission to a sociology graduate programme in the USA. A student's quantitative Graduate Record Examinations (GRE) score is an important selection criteria for admission as they must have a GRE score of at least 620 to be accepted. Only 34 students that had reached the threshold score were admitted; 209 students that had reached that score were not admitted because of reasons other than their GRE score, and 98 students that did not reach the 620 score were not admitted. However, one student that failed to reach the threshold score was admitted. Given this dataset, and knowing that the admitted student failed to reach the 620 score, would you recommend a student to take the risk of being like the exception? Would you advise the student to leave a score below 620 as it is, and to work on other factors that may contribute to admission success, e.g. by improving their score on the Test of English as a Foreign Language (TOEFL), improving their motivation letter or the recommendation letter from the supervisor? Or would you act as if the GRE level of 620 is necessary for admission, and advise the student to first make sure that their GRE score is at least 620?

Both the deterministic and the probabilistic view on necessity are legitimate, although the probabilistic view may be more realistic and pragmatic. The strength of the deterministic view is that this view denotes that the necessity applies to each single case in the theoretical domain. This makes the necessity logic very strong in practice. Without any exception the condition must be put and kept in place, and a necessary condition hypothesis can be falsified with a single case. However, with even a single exception, the deterministic view concludes that the condition is not necessary. As a consequence this view concludes that because of the exception it is not required to put and keep the condition in place for having the outcome. Although this is correct for the exceptional case, this is not correct for the vast majority of the cases. The probabilistic view, on the other hand, focuses on this vast majority of the cases and suggests that the condition must be put and kept in place to avoid a guaranteed failure in nearly all cases.

Causal logic versus conditional logic

The logic of necessary and sufficient causes is closely related to conditional logic in philosophy and mathematics dealing with statements like 'if A then B'. One main difference is that conditional logic is ignorant of the causal direction, whereas this is essential in causal logic, and thus NCA. One main characteristic of causality is that X and Y have a temporal order: first the cause X, then the effect Y. The symbols X and Y that conventionally refer to X as the cause and Y as the effect, are normally not used in conditional logic. Instead, in conditional logic A and B (or P and Q) are used to de-emphasise causality. In conditional logic four equivalent statements hold for the necessity of A for B. The first two statements are the same for causal necessity logic when A is the cause and B is the effect:

1. The presence of A is necessary for the presence of B.
2. The absence of A is sufficient for the absence of B.

In conditional logic, without a causal direction two additional equivalent statements hold:

3. The presence of B is sufficient for the presence of A.
4. The absence of B is necessary for the absence of A.

When A is opening this book and B is reading this book, the latter two statements are:

*   the presence of reading this book is sufficient for opening this book;
*   the absence of reading this book is necessary for the absence of opening this book.

Because opening the book comes before reading the book (opening the book is a necessary cause of reading the book) it is clear that the latter two conditional relations are not causal statements. In this book I only deal with the (assumed) causal relations between two concepts and therefore I use X for the cause and Y for the effect. When I use 'necessary' or 'necessary condition' I always mean 'necessary cause', hence when A causes B only the first two formulations of the necessary statements apply.

NECESSITY LOGIC BEYOND THE DICHOTOMOUS CASE

Until now I have presumed that X and Y are dichotomous and thus can have only two values: 0 and 1, absent or present, low or high. However, NCA's necessity logic can be extended to discrete and continuous variables that have more than two levels.

Necessary conditions for discrete and continuous variables

Figure 2.4 shows nine examples of necessary condition logic with various combinations of dichotomous, discrete (trichotomous) and continuous variables. The dichotomous necessary condition is shown in Figure 2.4A, which is the same as the ones shown in Figures 2.1B and 2.2A. *Dichotomous variables* can have only two values. This situation applies when the properties of the variables are considered inherently dichotomous, e.g. exam results (pass/fail), or are dichotomised, e.g. dividing countries into rich and poor based on a certain threshold level of Gross National Product (GDP). The values of the variables can be qualitative dichotomous scores (letters, words) such as M(ale) and F(emale), or quantitative dichotomous scores (numbers) such as 0 and 1. *Discrete variables* have a finite number of values (three or more). Variables with three levels are called 'trichotomous' variables. Some examples of inherently discrete variables are shoe sizes, days of the week, number of ideas in a suggestion box, or age in years. Again, variables can be discretised, and variable values can be quantitative or qualitative. *Continuous variables* can have an infinite number of values, e.g. temperature. Values of continuous variable are usually expressed as (rounded) numbers, possibly with decimals (e.g. 15.3). In NCA we assume that X and Y are bound and thus have minimum and maximum values. The bounds can be large but not infinite. The height of a person can be large but not infinite; innovation performance can be large but not infinite. In the plots of Figure 2.4 the minimum and maximum values of X and Y are standardised to 0 and 1. Hence, the dichotomous, discrete and continuous X and Y values can have two (dichotomous), a finite (discrete) or an infinite (continuous) number of levels between the bounds 0 and 1.

Figure 2.4A shows the 'dichotomous necessary condition' where X and Y are both dichotomous. In Figure 2.4B, X is discrete with three levels (trichotomous) and Y is dichotomous. In Figure 2.4C, X is continuous and Y is dichotomous. In Figure 2.4D, X is dichotomous and Y is discrete. Figure 2.4E shows the 'discrete necessary condition' where X and Y are both discrete. In Figure 2.4F, X is continuous and Y is

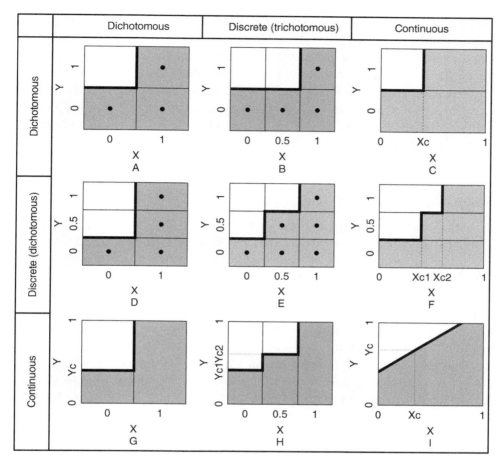

Figure 2.4   Nine types of necessary conditions depending on the levels of the variables

discrete. In Figures 2.4G and 2.4H, Y is continuous and X is dichotomous and dis-crete, respectively. Figure 2.4I shows the 'continuous necessary condition' where X and Y are both continuous.

Empty space, ceiling line, and effect size

In Figure 2.4 all plots have an empty space in the upper left corner. The borderline between the empty space where cases are (virtually) not possible, and the rest of the space where cases are possible, is called the *'ceiling line'*. In Figure 2.4 the ceiling lines are shown as thick lines.

The presence of an empty space could indicate that X is necessary for Y. This means that X constrains Y and that Y is constrained by X. The larger the empty space the larger the constraint that X poses on Y, and the more that Y is constrained by X. This constraint is called the necessity *'effect size'*. The effect size is the size of the empty space relative to the total space. The *'scope'* is the size of the total space given the minimum and maximum levels of X and Y. The effect size (d) is the empty space divided by the scope. The effect size can have values between 0 when there is no empty space, and 1 when the maximum possible space is empty. Chapter 4 includes a further explanation about the ceiling line, the effect size, and how that effect size can be calculated from data.

Necessity 'in kind' and 'in degree'

An empty space, and thus a necessity effect size > 0, may indicate the existence of a necessary condition 'in kind'. This is a qualitative statement about necessity, which can be formulated as 'X is necessary for Y'. When X or Y are discrete or continuous it is also possible to formulate a necessary condition 'in degree'. This is a quantitative statement about necessity, which can generally be formulated as 'level X is necessary for level Y'. In Figure 2.4B 'level 1 of X is necessary for level 1 of Y'. In Figure 2.4C at least level X_c is necessary for level 1 of Y. In Figure 2.4D level 1 of X is necessary for level 1 of Y. In Figure 2.4E at least level 0.5 of X is necessary for level 0.5 of Y, and level 1 of X is necessary for level 1 of Y. In Figure 2.4F at least level X_{c1} of X is necessary for level 0.5 of Y, and at least level X_{c2} of X is necessary for level 1 of Y. In Figure 2.4G level 1 of X is necessary for level $Y > Y_c$. In Figure 2.4H at least level $X = 0.5$ of X is necessary for level $Y > Y_{c1}$, and at least level 1 of X is necessary for level $Y > Y_{c2}$. When both X and Y are beyond dichotomous in one XY plot, several necessary condition statements 'in degree' may be formulated. In Figure 2.4I the ceiling line represents an infinite number of necessary conditions in degree depending on the point C on the ceiling line: $X \geq X_c$ is necessary for $Y = Y_c$. Point C basically dichotomises the X and Y variables at the cut-off point X_c and Y_c resulting in a dichotomous necessary condition as in Figure 2.1B. Another point on the ceiling line would produce another dichotomous necessary condition. By moving the point on the ceiling line the necessary condition changes in degree. Hence one could state that the ceiling line represents an infinite set of dichotomous necessary conditions.

Locations and shapes of the empty space

In Figure 2.4 the empty spaces are in the upper left corner. However, similar to dichotomous case (Figure 2.2) where the empty space can be in any corner depending on whether the absence or presence of X is necessary for absence or presence of Y, for the discrete and continuous cases the empty space can also be in any corner depending on whether low or high X is necessary for low or high Y. This is illustrated for the continuous necessary condition in Figure 2.5.

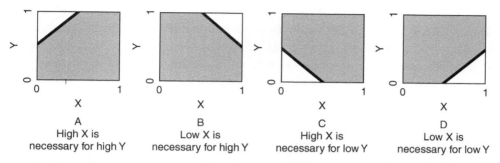

A	B	C	D
High X is necessary for high Y	Low X is necessary for high Y	High X is necessary for low Y	Low X is necessary for low Y

Figure 2.5 Four representations of continuous necessary condition 'X is necessary for Y' depending on whether low or high X is necessary for low or high Y

NECESSITY LOGIC IN PRACTICE AND RESEARCH

I claimed in Chapter 1 that necessity logic is everywhere. Practitioners often use necessity logic when they take action. For example, management consultants who want to advise organisations about change will not focus on all the possible factors that may influence change. They distinguish between 'must have' factors that must be present for successful change (thus necessary conditions) and 'nice to have' (or 'cool') factors that on average may influence change, but will not block success if absent ('contributing factors'). The absence of such contributing factors can be compensated by other factors. For example, the popular consultancy method called MoSCoW is a tool to prioritise factors for successful project management. M stands for 'Must haves', S for 'Should haves', C for 'Could haves', and W for 'Won't haves'. The 'Must haves' are the necessary conditions; the others are contributing factors. A 'Must have' 'describes a requirement that must be satisfied in the final solution for the solution to be considered a success' (International Institute of Business Analysis, 2009: 102). The MoSCoW method advises spending most of the time on the must have factors.

In practice, necessary conditions are many times called 'critical success factors' when the outcome is desired: factors that must be present for success. When the wording 'critical success factor' is used, its necessity meaning is usually implicit. However, here is an example of an explicit definition of the critical factor as a necessary condition:

Critical Success Factor (CSF) is a business term for an element which is necessary for an organization or project to achieve its mission. (Ranjan and Bhatnagar, 2008: 5)

Also, in research the wording 'critical success factor' and other alternative wordings for necessity (see Box 2.1) are routine, and the researcher may not always be aware of their logical meaning. However, the researcher may explicitly refer to necessity logic when using the words 'necessary condition' or 'necessary but not sufficient'. Goertz (2003) collected 150 examples of such statements in political science, and in past years I have collected a similar number of necessary condition statements in business and management research. Some examples from leading business and management journals are shown in Box 2.2 (emphasis added).

Box 2.2   Examples of 'necessary but not sufficient' statements in business and management research

- '... financial incentive is a **necessary but not sufficient condition** for motivating senior executives' (Pepper et al., 2013: 45).
- '... the ability of an entrepreneur to demonstrate previous performance is a **necessary, but not sufficient**, condition for success' (Treadway et al., 2013: 1536).
- '... knowledge assets are **necessary but not sufficient** to gain a competitive advantage' (Swart and Kinnie, 2010: 64).
- 'Managerial ties is **necessary, but not sufficient** for business success' (Peng and Luo, 2000).
- 'A unique set of knowledge and skills, receptivity to new ideas and opportunity recognition skills are all **necessary ingredients** for innovation' (De Winne and Sels, 2010: 1864).
- 'However, our contribution is to suggest that although these social relationships may be **necessary conditions** for high-performing cross-BU [Business Unit] collaborations, they are **not sufficient** conditions' (Martin and Eisenhardt, 2010: 293).
- '... higher quality HR management systems will become a **necessary, but not sufficient**, form of organizational infrastructure to provide a long term source of competitive advantage' (Huselid and Becker, 2010: 423).
- '... the reinforced trust stemming from the synergy of high perceived quality and a high level of CBI [Consumer-Brand Identification] constitutes a **necessary but not sufficient condition** for consumers to engage in identity-promoting behavior' (Lam et al., 2012: 312).
- '... a fertile relational context provides a **necessary, but not sufficient**, foundation for corporate venture unit survival' (Hill and Birkinshaw, 2014: 1907).

- 'While much prior research on absorptive capacity has only focused on the ability aspect of absorptive capacity, our results indicate that ability is **necessary but not sufficient**' (Minbaeva et al., 2014: 48).
- 'International coherence is a **necessary but not sufficient condition** for the realization of joint economies' (Celo and Chacar, 2015: 626).

One of the earlier examples is from Michael Porter's influential theory in his book *The Competitive Advantage of Nations* (1990). Although somewhat implicit, his theory is based on four necessary conditions for a nation's sustainable competitive success. Porter (1990: 74) says about the study on which his theory is based:

[the study] sought to separate the fundamental forces underlying national competitive advantage from the idiosyncratic ones.

Porter was searching for the common factors ('fundamental forces') in successful cases (nations with competitive advantage), and found four necessary conditions; he depicted these as the points of a diamond. The four conditions are: 'Factor Conditions', which are production factors such as skilled labour or infrastructure; 'Demand Conditions', related to the nature of the home-market for the home industries; 'Related and Supporting Industries', the presence in the nations of internationally competitive supplier and other related industries; and firm 'Strategy, Structure and Rivalry', about the conditions in the nation governing how companies are created, organised and managed, and the nature of the domestic rivalry. Porter (1990: 73) formulated the points of the diamond explicitly as necessary conditions as follows:

Advantages throughout the 'diamond' are necessary for achieving and sustaining competitive success in the knowledge-intensive industries that form the backbone of advanced economies.

It is clear that necessity logic is everywhere in research and practice. For a surprisingly long time, no tools existed for identifying necessary conditions in datasets. By adding NCA to the research toolbox new ways of analysing data have become possible, resulting in new theoretical and practical insights.

SUMMARY

In this chapter I presented the philosophical backgrounds of NCA concluding that most NCA research employs a positivist view, both in qualitative and quantitative research. This means that it is assumed 'there is a truth out there' that is investigated with NCA. I presented the underlying necessity logic of NCA, how this logic can be formulated, and how the necessity logic results in an expected data pattern between necessary condition X and the outcome Y. If the presence of X is necessary for the presence of Y, we can expect an empty space in the upper left corner of an XY table or scatter plot. I discussed the deterministic and the probabilistic views of necessity, as both are feasible. I also showed that the necessity logic can not only be applied to dichotomous variables that can have two levels, but also to discrete and continuous variables that can have more levels. This allows formulating the necessity condition by degree: 'level of X is necessary for level of Y'. Finally, I demonstrated that necessity logic is common in research and practice.

 **3**

BASIC COMPONENTS OF NCA

INTRODUCTION

In this chapter I discuss the basic components of NCA. These are theoretical statements (hypotheses), data, and data analysis. The goal of a hypothesis is to be explicit about the researcher's expectations regarding the necessity relationship between cause X and outcome Y. I discuss what theory is, what the core characteristics of theory are, and how a hypothesis stems from theory. The goal of data is to provide information about condition X and outcome Y from reality for finding evidence of necessity. I discuss how data can be collected in terms of research strategy, case selection and sampling, and measurement. This results in a dataset of scores to be analysed. The goal of data analysis is to use these scores to test the plausibility of the formulated necessity hypothesis. The three basic components of NCA are not unique for NCA as most research approaches have them. However, with NCA the operationalisation may be different. The hypothesis is based on necessity logic, the data are collected for finding evidence of necessity relations, and the data analysis for necessity is fundamentally different from traditional data analysis approaches. In this chapter I discuss each basic component by explaining it in general and highlighting the specifics for NCA. In Chapter 4 I describe NCA's data analysis approach in detail.

THEORETICAL STATEMENTS

Theory

'There is nothing as practical as a good theory' (Lewin, 1943: 129) and 'Bad theories are destroying good practice' (Groshal, 2005: 75). These statements indicate that with a good theory (a 'proven' theory) we can make predictions for any situation in the theoretical domain where that theory applies. But if the theory is not good, the predictions may be wrong. Usually it takes a long time to develop a theory and to test it empirically until we believe that the theory is supported enough to apply it. Hence, we do not 'prove' a theory, we can only make it more plausible by testing it over and over again until it is accepted by the relevant stakeholders as a 'true' theory. Thus, a single study can never prove a theory, but can 'only' give support to it or not. In the technical and medical sciences there are many 'proven' theories that are used fully in everyday life. 'Evidence-based practice', hence practising on the basis of theories that are empirically supported, is commonplace in engineering ('evidence-based engineering') and medicine ('evidence-based medicine'). The social sciences including business and management are less developed in this respect, e.g. 'evidence-based management' by management practitioners is still rare. The reason is that many theories in the social sciences are new and not yet fully developed and thoroughly tested. There are several reasons for this: first, the social sciences are relatively young in comparison to the technical and medical sciences; second, the social sciences are relatively small in comparison to the other sciences, including in terms of research funding; and third, the social sciences study complex, multi-causal social structures. Whereas in the natural sciences only a few variables can predict an outcome, in the social sciences with even tens of variables only a part of the outcome can be predicted. Einstein was able to predict nuclear energy with only two variables: mass and speed of light ($E = mc^2$), and the velocity of a car can be easily predicted from distance and time. Finney and Corbett (2007) found that at least 26 factors contribute to the successful implementation of business software; Evanschitzky et al. (2012) found that at least 20 factors contribute to successful new product development; and DeNeve and Cooper (1998) identified no less than 137 personality traits that contribute to subjective well-being. Yet only a part of the outcome can be explained with these factors. The interplay between many causal factors and how they contribute to the outcome is largely not yet understood. Research that includes many factors attempts to unravel this complexity.

NCA can reduce the complexity of social science theories by developing simpler theoretical statements that can be easily tested and retested. Rather than attempting to explain the *presence* of the outcome with a complexity of 'all' factors, which seems a mission impossible in the social sciences, NCA focuses on a few factors that really matter, not only for theory but also for practice. NCA concentrates on a single factor that can almost perfectly predict the *absence* of the outcome when it is absent: the necessary cause. NCA ignores the causality that predicts the presence of the outcome with a large number of factors. Consequently, NCA is not able, and does not attempt, to predict the presence of the outcome. NCA only makes relatively simple theoretical statements to predict the guaranteed absence of the outcome when the condition is absent. Such theoretical necessity statements can be easily developed and simply tested. For example, the theoretical claim that intelligence is necessary for creativity is simple and was developed by Guilford in 1967. It has only two factors: intelligence and creativity. Shortly after NCA became available, this theoretical statement was tested with NCA for the first time by Karwowski et al. (2016). Within a year the results were replicated in two other studies (Shi et al., 2017; Karwowski et al., 2017). This example shows that within a short time period, a necessity theoretical statement might gain support repeatedly, which could be the basis for evidence-based practice in terms of 'make sure that the necessary condition is in place, otherwise failure is inevitable'. Therefore, necessity theoretical statements can be relatively simple ('parsimonious') and are essential parts of a theory.

Propositions

The core of a theory is one or more 'propositions'. A proposition is a causal statement about the relationship between concepts. In its basic setup the proposition consists of two concepts and one theoretical relationship between these concepts. In the two conceptual models of Figure 3.1 (A and B) the concepts are represented by blocks, and the relationship by an arrow.

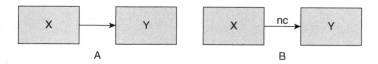

Figure 3.1   The relationship between a cause X and an effect Y.
A: unspecified relationship between X and Y. B: specified necessity relationship between X and Y.

Figure 3.1A represents the proposition 'X (the cause) has an effect on Y (the effect)'. A proposition is often formulated without giving much detail about the type of relationship between X and Y, other than a 'positive' or 'negative'. In conventional models, a 'positive' relationship implies that the presence or a high level of X produces on average the presence or a high level of Y. This represents sufficiency logic. However, the proposition 'X has an effect on Y' can also be interpreted with necessity logic: 'X (the cause) is necessary for Y (the effect)'. To emphasise the theoretical assumption of a necessary relationship between X and Y, the letters 'nc' (= **n**ecessary **c**ausal relation, or **n**ecessary **c**ondition relation) can be added to the arrow, as shown in Figure 3.1B.

Except for the concepts (X, Y) and their relationship (the proposition), two other important characteristics of the theory exist. However, these characteristics are often implicit and not formulated in the proposition and not visualised in the conceptual model. The two 'unseen' characteristics of a theory and thus a proposition are the 'focal unit' and the 'theoretical domain'. When you formulate a theoretical statement, I would advise you to formulate these characteristics explicitly also. The theory and thus the proposition apply to a certain *focal unit*. The specific focal unit depends on the phenomenon that is studied. When a researcher studies the relationship between a person's age (X) and a person's height (Y) the focal unit is 'person'. When a researcher studies the effect of a country's culture on a country's innovation performance, 'country' is the focal unit of interest. Other examples of focal units are 'employee', 'team', 'company', 'department', 'project', etc. A more complex focal unit is 'buyer-supplier relation', as in the study by Van der Valk et al. (2016) on the effect of contracts and trust on innovation performance. A single case study is research with one instance (case) of the focal unit of the theory, e.g. one person, one country or one team. In a small N study a small number of instances (cases) of the focal unit are selected for the research, and in a large N study a large number of instances (cases) of the focal unit are selected for the research. N is the number of cases of the focal unit that is selected for the particular research.

The concepts X and Y represent properties of the focal unit (e.g. age of a person) that must be measured for each selected case. Properties can be inherent parts of the focal unit (e.g. age of a person) or attributed to it (e.g. kindness of a person). A property can have different values (levels). Hence, a case is one instance, i.e. example or occurrence of the focal unit. When the focal unit is 'person', you are one instance of this focal unit, hence a case. Also you, your fellow readers, me, and every single human in the world are cases of this focal unit. However, the theory might not apply to all cases of the focal unit. The proposition that a person's height increases with a person's age does not apply to persons above a certain age.

The *theoretical domain* specifies the universe of instances of a focal unit where the theory and thus the proposition are supposed to hold. A proper specification of the theory therefore includes four elements: the concepts, the proposition, the focal unit and the theoretical domain.

Hypotheses

Until now I have talked in this chapter mainly about propositions, not about hypotheses. The words 'proposition' and 'concepts' indicate that we are talking about theory. The corresponding words 'hypothesis' and 'variables' indicate that we are talking about empirical reality. The hypothesis is the operationalisation of a theo-retical proposition in a specific empirical environment where it is tested or built. Similarly, a variable is the operationalisation of a theoretical concept that has a certain property that can be measured. The value (level, score) of this property (e.g. age) can vary, hence a 'variable'.

In this book I will use the words 'hypothesis' and 'variables' for a theoretical statement that is tested in an empirical reality. The focal unit and the theoretical domain of the theory also apply to the hypothesis and its variables. Thus, Figure 3.1 can be used to represent theory – a proposition showing the causal relationship between two concepts – or to represent the empirical reality – a hypothesis showing the causal relationship between two variables. The independent concept/variable (usually on the left) is the (presumed) cause X and the dependent concept/variable is the outcome Y. The arrow points from left to right to indicate the causal direction: first X then Y.

From now on, I will only talk about hypotheses. Thus, a hypothesis is a theoreti-cal claim about the relationships between variables for a certain focal unit in a certain theoretical domain. The researcher can claim, based on earlier research, practical experience, and logical reasoning etc., that a certain causal relationship between X and Y exists in reality. When a hypothesis states that two variables are associated (co-variation, correlation), it is not specified which variable causes the other; this may be represented by just a line between the two variables. In general we are interested in causality, hence the direction of the arrow. In the applied sci-ences, including business and management research, X is usually a variable that can be influenced in practice, and Y is a variable that is of interest in practice. All examples in Box 2.2 have one X that is manageable, one Y that is desired, and a presumed necessity causal relationship between X and Y.

Research that uses conventional data analysis, such as regression analysis, implic-itly assumes that the relationship between X and Y exists *on average*. The model predicts for a given X the average Y. Then the hypothesised relationship is claimed to hold for all cases combined together on average, not for each single case sepa-rately. Nevertheless, such hypotheses are commonly interpreted at case level as a hypothesis for 'the average case' or 'the typical case'. However, such cases are rela-tively rare. For example, it is rare to find an average company that has exactly the predicted average performance for a given X. By definition of the average and with the assumption of a normal distribution, half of the companies will have lower perfor-mance and half will have higher performance.

In NCA we deal with necessity logic and thus a necessity relationship between X and Y. The hypothesis claims that X is a necessary condition for Y. Rather than that X *produces* Y (on average), a necessity hypothesis states that X *enables* Y (allows Y) or that X *constrains* Y (is a bottleneck for Y) for practically every single case.

For average trend hypotheses, sometimes a positive or negative sign is added to the relationship. Then it is implied that X and Y have an increasing or decreasing relationship, usually a straight line: linear. A positive sign indicates that on average a higher value of X produces a higher value of Y: 'if X increases then it is likely that Y increases'. A positive sign also indicates that on average a lower value of X produces a lower value of Y: 'if X decreases then it is likely that Y decreases'. A negative sign indicates that on average a higher value of X produces a lower value of Y, and a lower value if X produces a higher value of Y. For necessity hypotheses adding a + or – sign does not make much sense. The type of necessity relationship should be specified differently.

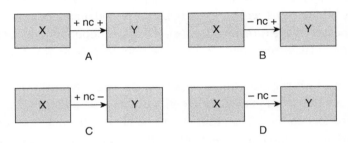

Figure 3.2   Representation of a necessary condition hypothesis describing the relationship between necessary cause X and outcome Y.
A: 'the presence or a high level of X is necessary for the presence or a high level of Y'.
B: 'the absence or a low level of X is necessary for the presence or a high level of Y'.
C: 'the presence or a high level of X is necessary for the absence or a low level of Y'.
D: 'the absence or a low level of X is necessary for the absence or a low level of Y'.

When the hypothesis is formulated in qualitative terms as 'X is a necessary condition for Y', and the letters 'nc' are added to the arrow, the hypothesis normally implies that the presence or a high level of X is necessary for the presence or a high level of Y. This interpretation could be emphasised by adding the symbol '+ nc +' to the arrow (Figure 3.2A). The '+' sign left of 'nc' refers to the presence or a high level of cause X, and the '+' sign on the right side of 'nc' refers to the presence or a high level of effect Y. It is also possible that the presence or a high level of X is necessary for the absence or a low level of Y (Figure 3.2C). This applies for example in the hypothesis 'the presence of social support is necessary for the absence of stress'. In this example, the symbol '+ nc –' can be added to the arrow. The '+' sign left of 'nc' refers to the presence or a high level of cause X, and the '–' sign on the right side of 'nc' refers to the absence or a low level of effect Y. Similarly, the symbols '– nc +' (Figure 3.2B) and '– nc –' (Figure 3.2D) are possible as well. When only 'nc' is used it can also mean that the researcher does not specify the presence or absence of X and Y in the hypothesis, possibly because they cannot make a claim about absence or presence of X for Y and the research is meant to explore the specific presumed necessity relationship.

It is possible that more than one variable is hypothesised to be necessary for an outcome. For example, Figure 3.3A shows a theoretical statement with two necessary conditions. Each arrow represents one necessity relationship.

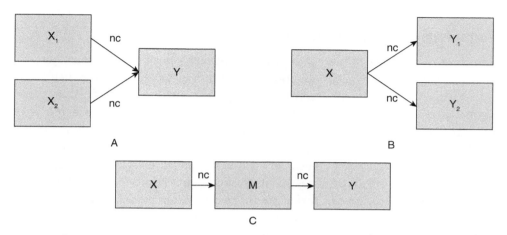

Figure 3.3 Example of conceptual models with necessity relationships.

A: Two necessary conditions X_i and one outcome Y; B: One necessary condition X and two outcomes Y_j; C: X is necessary for M and M is necessary for Y.

A necessary condition may also have an effect on two outcomes (Figure 3.3B). It is also possible that X is necessary for M, and M is necessary for Y (Figure 3.3C). In other words, M is a necessity mediator. M is an outcome for necessary condition X and M is a necessary condition for outcome Y. If X is necessary for M, and M is necessary for Y, then X is also necessary for Y. A necessary condition is not an inherent property of a variable but a role that the variable has in relation to other variables, as specified in the hypothesis. Any variable that is part of a complex causal 'average effect' model (e.g. in a multiple regression model or a structural equation model) could (theoretically) also have a role as necessary condition. It is also possible that none of the factors in a complex causal 'average effect' model are necessary.

Most hypotheses are qualitative binary statements. For example, the theoretical claim 'X on average has a positive effect on Y' can be tested with regression analysis. The answer to whether this hypothesis holds is yes/no depending on whether the slope of the regression line is zero or not (and on whether the result is statistically significant or not). The qualitative binary theoretical claim that 'X is necessary for Y' can be tested with NCA. The answer is yes/no depending on whether a ceiling line exists and the effect size is above a certain threshold (and on wheter the result is statistically significant). Such a qualitative binary hypothesis is therefore called an 'in kind' hypothesis where the regression line or ceiling line is not specified in the hypothesis. In a hypothesis 'in degree' the expected regression or ceiling line is speci-fied. The majority of average effect hypotheses and necessary condition hypotheses are formulated as 'in kind' hypotheses.

Formulating hypotheses for NCA

Empirical researchers in the social sciences including business and management are usually expected to make a theoretical contribution and to formulate their theo-retical expectations explicitly before they collect and analyse data for testing these statements, at least in the positivist framework. Because 'for any research area one can find important necessary condition hypotheses' (Goertz and Starr, 2003: 65–66), it can be relatively easy to formulate theoretical necessity statements in your field of research. I distinguish between four types of existing necessity state-ments: explicitly formulated necessity statements that are broadly accepted in the research community; explicitly formulated necessity statements that are not broadly accepted in the research community; implicitly formulated and non-accepted neces-sity statements; and new necessity statements. With 'explicitly formulated' I mean that the words 'necessary', 'necessity' or 'necessary condition' etc. are used to refer to the causal relationship. With 'implicitly formulated' I mean that words that hint at necessity logic but do not use the words 'necessary', 'necessity' or 'necessary con-dition' etc. are used to refer to the causal relationship (see Box 2.1). With 'accepted necessity statements' I mean that it is clear that the research community discuss-ing the statement accepts the necessity logic. With 'not broadly accepted necessity statements' I mean that it is clear that the research community discussing the state-ment does not use necessity logic, but instead uses logic based on contributing factors and average trends.

Explicitly formulated and accepted theoretical necessity statements are rare. One example is the accepted necessity statement that intelligence is necessary for creativity that was originally proposed by Guilford in 1967 and has since been broadly adopted in the psychology of intelligence and creativity research community. Because the theoretical statement is already explicitly formulated with necessity logic, and because the statement is already broadly accepted, there is not much need for further theoretical arguments on why it is worthwhile to test this hypothesis with NCA. Karwowski et al. (2016), Shi et al. (2017) and Karwowski et al. (2017) have tested this hypothesis with NCA. You can make an important contribution by testing a well-established and broadly accepted theoretical necessity statement with NCA for the first time, or again. However, well-established and broadly accepted theoreti-cal necessity statements are sporadic.

Explicitly formulated but non-accepted theoretical necessity statements are more common. Examples of these statements are in Box 2.2. Also Porter's (1990) theory on the competitive advantage of nations, the four 'diamond factors', has an explicitly formulated necessary condition statement, but Porter's theory is not known for being a necessary condition theory, and the diamond factors are treated as factors that contribute on average to competitive performance. In such a case you can make an important contribution by highlighting the necessity statements that are formulated, and by emphasising the logical arguments for the necessity nature of the relationship, which justifies testing them with NCA.

Implicitly formulated and not broadly accepted theoretical necessity statements may be even more common. Social science theories that attempt to predict the outcome with multiple predictors focus on average trends. Nevertheless, theoretical statements are also often made that hint at necessity logic using wording like the examples shown in Box 2.1. You can make an important contribution by making an implicitly suggested necessity relation explicit by giving logical arguments for the necessity nature of the relationship between X and Y, beyond the importance of the relationship on average, and apply NCA to test the necessity hypothesis. In particular you can argue why the outcome cannot be present without the condition, and why the absence of the condition cannot be compensated by other factors.

Testing explicitly or implicitly existing theoretical necessity statements is not only efficient for the researcher, as they can be selected from the literature, it is also a valuable contribution to research and practice. Existing theoretical necessity statements may have been formulated in earlier research, but may not have been tested empirically (with data). Furthermore, existing and unproved statements may be widely used in practice ('necessity theory in use'), but may not have been tested. Testing untested theoretical statements is a valuable contribution to research and practice. Even if the theoretical statement has already been tested before, adding another test is also a valuable contribution because it is only after many replications that confidence can be gained for the theoretical statement being 'true'. In the social sciences replication studies are not (yet?) as much performed as in the technical and medical sciences. Many gatekeepers within research, such as supervisors, peers, and journal editors, expect researchers and research projects to produce novel theoretical contributions, and retesting existing theoretical statements is commonly less valued as a contribution than developing and testing new theoretical statements.

Finally, you can develop your own, *new theoretical necessary condition statement*. One way of doing this is by evaluating whether a factor that contributes to an outcome on average could also be a necessary condition. Evaluating contributing factors from previous research and the mechanisms for how they contribute to the outcome can inspire NCA researchers to suggest that a contributing factor could also be necessary for the outcome. For example, Van der Valk et al.'s (2016) research, and the research of Knol et al. (2018), build on existing theories. Van der Valk et al. (2016) noticed that in existing research, 'contract detail' is considered an important contributing factor *on average* for successful innovation performance in buyer and supplier collaboration. They introduced the *necessity* hypothesis for the relationship between having detailed contracts and innovation success, and tested this hypothesis with NCA. Similarly, Knol et al. (2018) found in existing research that management commitment is important *on average* for successful lean production, and formulated the necessary condition hypothesis that management commitment is *necessary* for successful lean production and tested this hypothesis with NCA. Hence, you can make an important contribution by being the first to formulate a necessary conditions statement for an XY relationship that has only been formulated and tested using average effect methodologies, e.g. with multiple regression analysis or structural equation modelling. The mechanism for why X is important for Y (on average) may already have been explained. What you can add here is to argue that X is not only important on average, but is also necessary, without compensation possibilities. Hence, it is relatively easy to extend existing theories by assuming a necessity relationship between certain concepts of the theory and the outcome. Any concept with any role in an average trend model, such as the role of independent concept, moderator concept, or mediator concept, can be a candidate for being a necessary condition, when there is theoretical support for it. The concept is then not only an important contributing factor to the outcome on average, but also a necessary condition for the outcome.

It is also possible to consider the dimensions of overarching 'latent concepts' that are used in existing models as separate potential necessary conditions. For example, the latent concept of a person's 'happiness' may consist of several dimensions, such as 'happiness with family' and 'happiness with work'. Even if the combined concept 'happiness' may not be considered as a necessary condition, one or more separate dimensions could be necessary for the outcome. Your theoretical statement can be formulated either in terms of X being an enabling factor for Y, by using the enabling wording examples in Box 2.1, or in terms of X being a constraining factor for Y, by using the constraining wording examples in Box 2.1. In Appendix 1, I give further suggestions for how you can develop a new necessary condition hypothesis when you have only formulated a general research topic or general research question.

DATA

The next basic component of NCA is the data to be used for the analysis of necessary conditions. Although 'data analysis' rather than 'data' is the focus of NCA, the quality of the data analysis depends on the quality of the data. I shall therefore explain shortly what I mean by good data, how this is a prerequisite for an NCA analysis, and how the results of NCA can be biased by bad data. The quality of the data depends on the choice of the *research strategy* (experimental study, small N observational study, or large N observational study), how the cases are *selected or sampled* (purposive sampling, probability sampling, convenience sampling), how valid and reliable the *measurements* are, and how the *dataset* for an NCA data analysis is organised. I discuss these elements below.

Research strategy

'Research strategy' (or 'research design') refers to the type of research that is used to test the necessary condition hypothesis. The main categories of research strategy are the experiment and the observational study. In the *experiment* the independent variable is manipulated by the researcher in a laboratory or in the field and the effect of this manipulation on the outcome is observed. All other factors but the manipulated factors are controlled or assumed constant such that a change in the dependent variable can be causally attributed to the change of the independent variable. The gold standard of the experiment is the randomised control trial (RCT) whereby cases are randomly assigned to a 'control group', in which the independent variable is not manipulated, and a 'treatment group', in which the independent variable is manipulated. By comparing the outcomes of the two groups a conclusion can be drawn about the causal effect of the manipulation on the outcome. The experiment is considered the best research strategy for making causal inference from the positivist's perspective, as it is best equipped for making causal interpretations of the results.

In the usual experiment, X and Y are absent or have low levels. Then the X of the treatment group is manipulated by increasing its value and it is observed if the expected effect on Y (increase) occurs in the treatment group compared to the control group. This is a sufficiency experiment: X produces Y. Usually it is observed if X has an average effect on Y in the group of cases. In the necessity experiment X and Y are present or have high levels. Then X in the treatment group is manipulated by decreasing it and it is observed if the expected effect on Y (lower) occurs in the treatment group compared to the control group. It is expected that the effect will occur in practically every case. For example, in an imaginary necessity field experiment two similar and successful departments of a company are studied. Both departments have a strong leader, and this is hypothesised to be a critical success factor or necessary condition for success. In the field experiment the strong leader in one group is taken away and replaced by a weak leader. The success of both departments is measured after some time, and the researcher evaluates if the success of the department with the weak leader (treatment group) has declined in comparison to the success of the department with the strong leader (control group). If so, support is found for the necessity hypothesis. Figure 2.4G could represent the data of this experiment where $X = 0$ corresponds to a weak leader, $X = 1$ to a strong leader, $Y = 1$ to department success, and $Y = Y_c$ to declined department success.

In business and management, the experiment is often not the first choice for prag-matic reasons. The manipulation of X may not be possible, desirable, or practical. Nevertheless, it is worthwhile to consider using an experiment strategy for NCA and reflect on what such an experiment would look like. I have two reasons for this sug-gestion. First, many researchers too quickly state that an experiment is not possible in their situation. After careful consideration it may be possible anyway. Second, if the researcher does not choose to do an experiment but instead performs an obser-vational study, they can be explicit about the reasons for not doing an experiment and can report those reasons when discussing the limitations of the observational study as regards causal interpretations. A common disadvantage of the experiment in an average trend, sufficiency-based experiment is that only a few variables and a limited number of levels of those variables can be manipulated. This is a disadvan-tage because an additive sufficiency model with only a few variables usually poorly predicts the presence of the outcome, as many factors contribute to the outcome. This disadvantage counts less for NCA because NCA is interested in the necessity effect of single variables and the absence of a single variable is a good predictor of the absence of the outcome.

Currently, most studies in business and management are *observational studies*. The observational study does not manipulate variables but keeps the real-life con-text as it is. Compared to an experiment an observational study has more 'ecological validity', meaning that the results may be better generalisable and applicable in multi-causal real-life settings. The observational research strategy for NCA is not dif-ferent from any other observational research strategy. In an observational study, it is more difficult to make a causal interpretation of an observed relationship between X and Y. The causal interpretation highly depends on theoretical support. An obser-vational study can be categorised into a small N observational study (such as a case study) and large N observational study (such as a survey study). N is the number of cases that are selected for the study. The difference between a small N study and a large N study is not just the number of cases (N) that are studied. In a small N study the researcher has more opportunities to take the complex environment into account. A small N study can be a single case study, or a study of a small number of cases (comparative case study). In a large N observational study the researcher has the opportunity to generalise the results and perform a statistical analysis.

Case selection (sampling)

A case is a single instance (example) of the focal unit of a theory. When the focal unit is employee (of a company), the employee and not the company is the case. To obtain data cases must be selected. Case selection (sampling) is an important choice for any study. The cases must be selected from the theoretical domain because the hypothesis is supposed to hold within that domain. For example, the defined theoretical domain of the hypothesis that age has an effect on height may be young persons under the age of 20 years. It then makes no sense to select a person who is 45 years old. The square in Figure 3.4 represents the domain of a theory where each dot is a case. For small N observational studies, the cases are usually selected with a certain purpose from the theoretical domain. This type of case selection is called 'purposive sampling'. For small N NCA, for example cases with high level of the outcome can be selected purposively to test whether these cases have high level of the condition, thus to test whether the upper left corner is empty or not. When cases with high Y and low X are observed (thus cases in the empty space), the necessary condition hypothesis is falsified. In other words, cases must be selected such that this expected empty space can be evaluated of being empty or not.

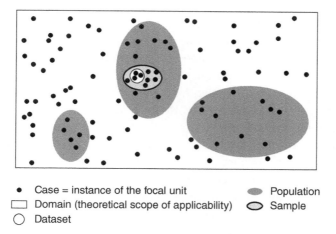

•	Case = instance of the focal unit		Population
▢	Domain (theoretical scope of applicability)	⬭	Sample
◯	Dataset		

Figure 3.4   The theoretical domain of cases where the hypothesis is assumed to hold showing three populations, one sample and one dataset
(Adapted from: Dul and Hak, 2008).

This is an option particularly when the outcome is a dichotomous variable (absent/present, low/high, failure/success, 0/1, etc.). Purposive case selection can be done in two ways. The first possibility is to select cases where the outcome is present, thus successful cases, and to test whether the space in the upper left corner is empty or not. This is called case selection on the basis of the presence of the dependent variable (Dion, 1998). Because successful cases all share the presence of the outcome, e.g. all pregnant persons are woman, or all successful organisational change projects have senior management commitment, such cases can be used to falsify the hypothesis that the condition is necessary for the presence of the outcome. Finding a case of successful organisational change without management commitment falsifies the necessary condition hypothesis (in the deterministic view on necessity).

Selecting cases where the outcome is present might be efficient when the researcher can estimate relatively easily the case's presence of the outcome before the formal measurement is made. For example, in a small N study with 10 nations, Porter selected only successful trading nations to find necessary conditions for success. The second possibility of case selection for necessity testing is to select cases where the condition is absent and test whether the space in the upper left corner is empty or not. The first approach is usually more efficient than the second. When the outcome variable has more than two levels, purposive selection becomes more complex and might not be practical.

For necessity testing in a large N study, a 'population' of cases within the theoretical domain must be selected. Normally the theoretical domain from which the population is chosen is not homogeneous. Thus, within the theoretical domain populations may have different characteristics. For a large N study, a 'census study' would be optimal: selecting all cases from the population such that the necessity theory about the population can be directly tested. It is then not necessary to take a sample from the population and statistically generalise from the sample to the population, and hence, there is no need for inferential statistics. In practice, however, populations are often large, such that it is difficult to obtain a census. In this situation a sample of cases is drawn from the population to represent that population. This sample can only represent the population from which it is drawn, not the entire theoretical domain. For statistical inference, i.e. statistical generalisation from the sample to the population, it is necessary to select a *probability sample*. For example, the commonly encouraged *random sample* ensures that all cases from the population have an equal chance to be part of the sample. A random sample can be obtained by randomly drawing cases from a list ('sampling frame') of all cases in the population. However, not all of the selected cases from a population may show up in the dataset, e.g. when companies from a population of companies were invited to participate in a study but actually did not participate, and this may result in 'non-response bias'. The statistical generalisation from a sample to a population may be biased when the researcher selects a *convenience sample*, which is selecting cases for convenience, e.g. companies that the researcher has access to. Selecting a sample for convenience is methodologically undesirable because of the potential bias when generalising from sample to population. A convenience sample only allows for making statements about the sample, not about the population. Statistical generalisation from a sample to the *theoretical domain* is not possible with any sample (unless the theoretical domain equals the population, e.g. when the domain is small and a sampling frame is available for it). Generalisation to the domain is only possible with replication studies with other cases (small N) or other populations (large N). For example, in meta-analyses results from several studies are combined to make theoretical statements beyond single populations in a larger part of the theoretical domain.

However, in the social sciences samples are seldom true probability samples (resulting in sampling bias). Furthermore, it is usually only a small part of the cases that were selected for being part of the sample that end up in the dataset, resulting in non-response bias. In many research projects, convenience sampling rather than probability sampling is done, and non-response is usually relatively large, commonly above 50% (e.g. Baruch and Holtom, 2008). These limitations should be acknowledged, and over-valuing the results of inferential statistics should be avoided. The results describe the sample of cases but can possibly not be generalised beyond this sample. These sampling issues are not unique for NCA. Any data analysis method needs a good sample that is representative of the population to which the researcher wants to generalise the results. Replications are needed as well.

Measurement

After cases are selected each case is approached for measurement to obtain scores for the X and Y variables. A score is a value that is assigned to a variable based on data. Data are recordings of evidence generated in the process of data collection. For example, when data are collected with a questionnaire, a subject can give numbers to a rating scale, such as a five-point Likert scale from 1 to 5. These numbers are *data*. By combining these numbers, *scores* of variables can be obtained. For example, when a variable is measured by three questions or items, the mean value of the numbers that are given by the subject may be used as the score of the variable. When the *rating scale* has five levels from 1 to 5, the score of the variable ranges from 1 to 5 as well (from $3/3 = 1$ to $15/3 = 5$) but has 13 levels, namely 3/3, 4/3, 5/3, ... 13/3, 14/3, 15/3. In general, scores can have two values (dichotomous), three or more values (discrete), or a large number of values up to infinity (continuous).

The quality of the measurement is mainly determined by two aspects: reliability and validity. Reliability relates to the precision of the measurement. If the same researcher or another researcher were to repeat the measurement the same scores should be obtained; if this is not the case the measurement is not reliable. Validity relates to the question if the researcher measures what was supposed to be measured. If this is not the case the scores are not valid. When you use existing data for your study, you accept the quality of the existing data. Although you cannot influence the quality of the data, knowing the data quality in terms of reliability and validity is helpful for understanding the strengths and weaknesses of your research.

Measurement scores can be obtained by using a variety of measurement approaches such as observation, questionnaire, interview, 'hard' measurement with instruments, etc. The goal is to score the value of a property of the case that is of interest (X, Y). The variables that must be measured are the variables of the hypothesis. Sometimes researchers will collect additional data for other uses or for exploration afterwards, but the data collection must focus on the quality of the measurement of the variables of the hypothesis.

A detailed discussion about measurement is beyond the scope of this book.

Dataset

After the measurement, the data must be organised and stored in a dataset, although a better name for dataset would be a 'set of scores'. Figure 3.5 shows a typical format for an Excel dataset for research data, which can also be used in NCA. Each row is a case, except for the first row that is a header with column names. Each column is a variable, except for the first column that has the row names. Details of this dataset are discussed in the chapter 'Data Analysis with NCA', section 'Example dataset' below (p.45).

	A	B	C	D
1	Case	Individualism	Risk taking	Innovation performance
2	Australia	90	84	50.9
3	Austria	55	65	52.4
4	Belgium	75	41	75.1
5	Canada	80	87	81.4
6	Czech Rep	58	61	14.5
7	Denmark	74	112	116.3
8	Finland	63	76	173.1
9	France	71	49	77.6
10	Germany	67	70	109.5
11	Greece	35	23	12
12	Hungary	80	53	5.4
13	Ireland	70	100	62.3
14	Italy	76	60	19.7

Figure 3.5 Example of a dataset showing 13 cases (countries) and three variables (Individualism, Risk taking, Innovation performance)

DATA ANALYSIS

Data analysis is at the core of NCA. Its main goal is to test a necessity hypothesis by analysing the dataset. Hypothesis testing is comparing the data pattern that is expected when the hypothesis holds, with the observed data pattern ('pattern matching'). Expected data patterns for different types of necessity conditions are shown in Figure 2.4 for different levels of the X and Y variables. For necessity hypotheses in which 'the presence or a high level of X is necessary for the presence or a high level of Y' an empty space in the upper left corner of an XY plot can be expected. For necessity hypotheses that are formulated in terms of 'absence' or 'a low level' of X or Y the empty space is expected in another corner as shown in Figure 2.2 and Figure 2.5. The data analysis consists of evaluating whether the actual data show that the space that is expected to be empty actually is empty, quantifying the size and accuracy of the empty space, and evaluating if the empty space may be the result of random chance (statistical significance test). As I will show in Chapter 4, the data analysis needs the following steps:

- Step 1: Make the graphical representation of the XY relation: XY contingency table or XY scatter plot.
- Step 2: Identify the empty space.
- Step 3: Draw the ceiling line.
- Step 4: Quantify the NCA parameters.
- Step 5: Evaluate the NCA parameters.
- Step 6: Formulate the conclusion.

The data analysis results in a statement whether or not the hypothesis is rejected or supported. Researchers may be disappointed that a hypothesis has been rejected. However, the goal of hypothesis testing is not to confirm the hypothesis, but rather to try to falsify it. Whereas a confirmation just finds what was expected, a rejection of a hypothesis is a valuable result with potentially interesting lessons. A hypothesis can be rejected for at least four reasons:

- The measurement was not valid or reliable. Measurement error or other methodological errors may have caused the rejection of the hypothesis, although the hypothesis may still hold.
- The hypothesis is rejected in only a part of the theoretical domain, i.e. the part where it was tested. The hypothesis may still hold for other parts of the domain.
- The rejection may be the result of random chance; with another sample the hypothesis may not be rejected.
- The rejection may indicate that the hypothesis and underlying theory are not correct.

The last conclusion is strong. The researcher had a good theoretical reason to formulate the hypothesis. Such a strong conclusion about the incorrectness of the hypothesis and underlying theory can only be made when the other reasons for rejection are excluded. It is usually only after many replications in the same and different parts of the domain that more definite conclusions can be drawn about the generic correctness of a hypothesis and its theory. Hence, a humble attitude is appropriate when presenting the results of a single study. A well-performed single empirical study adds to our knowledge about the theoretical necessity statement, but more definite conclusions can only be drawn when the results of different studies are combined, e.g. in a (future) meta-analysis. This is true for any data analysis method. Chapter 4 discusses the details of NCA's data analysis approach.

SUMMARY

In this chapter I presented the three basic components of NCA: theoretical statements (hypotheses), data and data analysis. A hypothesis represents the researcher's expectation about the necessity of condition X for outcome Y. The hypothesis can be tested by purposefully selecting cases in a small N study, or by drawing a random sample in a large N study. For proper data analysis, valid and reliable scores of X and Y must be available for all cases. These scores can be obtained from an existing dataset or from new data based on new measurements. In the data analysis the hypothesis is tested.

4

DATA ANALYSIS WITH NCA

INTRODUCTION

In this chapter I guide you step by step through NCA's data analysis approach. I presume that you have formulated one or more necessary condition hypotheses, and that you have a dataset to test these hypotheses (see Chapter 3). I distinguish between data analysis with the 'contingency table approach', consisting of a qualitative analysis of the data by visual inspection, and data analysis with the 'scatter plot approach', consisting of a quantitative analysis of the data with the NCA software. The contingency table approach can be useful when you have a dataset with X and Y scores that have a small number of levels (up to five), e.g. in a small N study. The scores can be qualitative such as words (e.g. Low, Medium, High) or letters (e.g. L, M, H), but these levels can also be coded as numbers (e.g. 0, 0.5, 1). The scatter plot approach can be useful when you have a dataset with X and Y scores that have a large number of levels (more than five) and when the scores are numbers, for example in a large N study.

I will illustrate the required steps for each of the two approaches with an example. First, I will introduce the example dataset that is used in both approaches.

EXAMPLE DATASET

In the example I test the hypothesis that a high level of a country's individualism is necessary for a country's innovation performance. Hence, the focal unit is 'country', and the variables are Individualism (X) and Innovation performance (Y). I test this hypothesis in one population, namely the population consisting of Western countries. Western countries are defined as countries that were shaped historically by Western Christianity, use the Latin alphabet, and have similar cultural and ethical values (Huntington, 1993). The approximate size of this population is 70 countries. I obtained a convenience sample by selecting 25 Western countries for which scores are available for Individualism and Innovation performance. The scores for Individualism are from Hofstede (1980) and the scores for Innovation performance from Gans and Stern (2003). For illustrating the contingency table approach, I selected a subset of seven countries from this sample of 25 countries. The two Excel datasets to illustrate NCA with the contingency approach and with the scatter plot approach are shown in Figure 4.1A and Figure 4.1B, respectively. The dataset for illustration of the contingency table approach (Figure 4.1A) has seven cases for which X and Y are dichotomised (Low and High). I obtained these qualitative variable scores by using the cut-off value of 50 for Individualism and 100 for Innovation performance. The dataset for illustration of the scatter plot

	A	B	C
1	Case	Individualism	Innovation performance
2	Australia	90	50.9
3	Austria	55	52.4
4	Belgium	75	75.1
5	Canada	80	81.4
6	Czech Rep	58	14.5
7	Denmark	74	116.3
8	Finland	63	173.1
9	France	71	77.6
10	Germany	67	109.5
11	Greece	35	12
12	Hungary	80	5.4
13	Ireland	70	62.3
14	Italy	76	19.7
15	Mexico	30	1.2
16	Netherlands	80	68.7
17	New Zealand	79	14.9
18	Norway	69	75.1
19	Poland	60	3.5
20	Portugal	27	11.1
21	Slovak Rep	52	3.5
22	Spain	51	17.3
23	Sweden	71	184.9
24	Switzerland	68	149.7
25	UK	89	79.4
26	USA	91	214.4

	A	B	C
1	Case	Individualism	Innovation performance
2	Finland	High	High
3	France	High	Low
4	Greece	Low	Low
5	Italy	High	Low
6	Portugal	Low	Low
7	Switzerland	High	High
8	UK	High	Low

A   B

Figure 4.1   Example datasets for testing the hypothesis that a country's Individualism (X) is necessary for a country's Innovation performance (Y).

A: small dataset of seven cases for illustrating the 'contingency table approach'. B: larger dataset of 25 countries for illustrating the 'scatter plot approach'.

approach (Figure 4.1B) has all 25 cases, and X and Y are (nearly) continuous with many levels. For each dataset in Figure 4.1, the first column contains the case names (countries), the second column has the scores for Individualism, and the third column has the scores for Innovation performance.

DATA ANALYSIS WITH THE CONTINGENCY TABLE APPROACH

The 'contingency table approach' consists of the following six steps:

- Step 1: Make the contingency table.
- Step 2: Identify the empty space.
- Step 3: Draw the ceiling line.
- Step 4: Quantify the NCA parameters.
- Step 5: Evaluate the NCA parameters.
- Step 6: Formulate the conclusion.

Step 1: Make the contingency table

First you need to make a contingency table. This is a table in matrix format where each cell represents a combination of the X and Y values that were observed in a case. Figure 4.2 shows the contingency table of the example dataset (Figure 4.1A). This contingency table has four cells because X and Y each have two levels. The two levels of X and Y are coded qualitatively as Low and High. The X values are 'horizontal' and the Y values are 'vertical', and values increase 'to the right' and 'upward'. The total number of cells in the table equals the multiplication of the number of levels of X and the number of levels of Y. When X and Y each have two levels, and thus are dichotomous variables, the total number of cells of the contingency table is four; when X and Y each have three levels the total number of cells of the contingency table is nine. In each cell you must write the number of cases that have that particular combination of X and Y values. Figures 2.1, 2.2, and 2.4 (A,B,D,E) are examples of contingency tables, but without any specification for the number of cases per cell.

The reason for making a contingency table is that you can compare the observed data pattern with the expected data pattern when X is necessary for Y ('pattern matching'). The expected pattern depends on how you define your necessary condition hypothesis. If you define your hypothesis as 'the presence of or a high level of X is necessary for the presence of or high level of Y', which is the default expression in this book, then you can expect a contingency table with empty cells in the upper left corner.

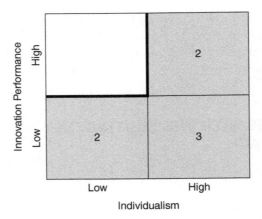

Figure 4.2 The contingency table for the dataset of Figure 4.1A with seven cases for testing – by falsification – the hypothesis that a country's individualism is necessary for a country's innovation performance. The hypothesis is not falsified by the seven cases because as expected, the upper left corner is empty.

Step 2: Identify the empty space

In the second step you need to visually inspect the contingency table to check whether an empty space exists in the expected corner. Three situations can apply. First, *the expected empty space is empty*. The condition may be necessary because no observation shows that it is possible to have the outcome without the condition. You must then continue the analysis with Step 3. Second, *the expected empty space is clearly not empty*. A large number of cases (e.g. > 5%) are present in the expected empty space. The condition may then not be necessary because the observations show that it is possible to have the outcome without the condition. Hence, the analysis results in a rejection of the necessary condition hypothesis and continues with Step 6. Third, *the expected empty space is almost empty*. It has a few outliers. An outlier is a case that is considered to be 'far away' from the other cases. You can evaluate outliers in three ways.

First, the outlier can be caused by an *error*. This error can be due to measurement error or to sample error. When the outlier has measurement error this error must be corrected, or the outlier must be removed from the dataset. When the outlier is due to sample error, it does not belong to the theoretical domain or the population, and so the case is outside the scope of the study. For example, when the hypothesis is about Western countries and the case is a non-Western country, then the case should not be used for testing this hypothesis, and should be removed. If all the outliers in the otherwise empty space have errors and are removed you must continue with Step 3. You should always justify and report the removal of outliers.

The second way to evaluate an 'almost' empty space is to consider the outliers as exceptions for unknown reasons. You may have adopted a *probabilistic* view on necessity (see chapter 'Philosophical Assumptions and Logic of NCA', section 'Deterministic and probabilistic views on necessity' , p.17) and are willing to accept a relatively small number of outliers (e.g. ≤ 5%) in the otherwise empty space. You can then continue the analysis while accepting some cases as outliers. A possible necessary condition is reported as a probabilistic necessary condition, e.g. as 'almost always necessary'.

The third way to evaluate an 'almost' empty space is to consider the presence of even one case in this space as the reason for rejecting the hypothesis. You have now adopted a *deterministic* view on necessity. Even a single case in the 'empty' space shows that the outcome is possible without the condition, presuming that there is no measurement or sample error in this case. Hence, the researcher continues the analysis with Step 6.

Box 4.1 shows an example of a single outlier that was observed in the corner that was expected to be empty.

Box 4.1   Outlier in the GRE example

The GRE example was discussed in Chapter 2 (see Figure 2.3) showing that 342 students applied for admission to a sociology graduate programme and that the student must have a GRE score of at least 620 for admission. However, an outlier was observed in the upper left corner of the contingency table. The outlier is a student who had a low GRE score and was admitted. Could this outlier be the result of measurement error? This error did not apply: the outlier student was indeed admitted and had a low GRE score. Could the case be the result of sample error? Probably not because the outlier student was a normal student who could be admitted to the programme and had done the GRE test. When the reason for the outlier is unknown a researcher who has a deterministic view on necessity will reject the hypothesis. However, a researcher who has a probabilistic view may accept the hypothesis and formulate it as 'A high GRE score is almost always necessary for Admission'.

The GRE example shows the value of falsifying a hypothesis as follows. In general a rejection of a hypothesis is more informative than an acceptance. In the probabilistic view on necessity the hypothesis was accepted according to the expectation. In the deterministic view the hypothesis was rejected against the expectation. A rejection triggers searching for the reasons why the hypothesis was rejected. Why was this student an outlier? It turns out (Vaisey, personal communication, July 2, 2014) that the outlier student was admitted based on a faculty member's explicit testimony as to the student's quantitative abilities, which was regarded as superior information to the quantitative GRE score. This information allows the formulation of a more precise theoretical domain for the hypothesis: the hypothesis only applies to students who enter the programme via the formal selection rules.

In the example of individualism and innovation performance, the expected empty space in the upper left corner is empty (situation 1). Hence, the analysis continues with Step 3.

Step 3: Draw the ceiling line

You will have to continue with Step 3 if the expected empty space is indeed empty or if you accept some outliers in this 'empty' space. Because the 'empty' space may include some cases, this space is renamed as the 'ceiling zone'. The ceiling zone is the size of the 'empty' zone in the corner that was expected to be empty. In this step you literally or imaginarily draw a line that separates the cells in the ceiling zone from the rest of the cells of the contingency table. Drawing the ceiling line is a preparation for the next step in which the NCA parameters are calculated.

In Figure 4.2 the ceiling line is the thick step line with a horizontal part and a vertical part.

Step 4: Quantify the NCA parameters

In Step 4 several NCA parameters are calculated. The main parameters are the necessity 'effect size', and the accuracy that the empty space is indeed empty ('ceiling accuracy or *c*-accuracy'). In order to calculate these parameters, other parameters must be calculated first.

Scope The scope is the total space where X and Y values can be expected given the minimum and maximum values of X and Y. There are two options for defining the scope: the empirical scope and the theoretical scope. The empirical scope is based on the *observed* minimum and maximum values of X and Y in the dataset. The theoretical scope is based on the *theoretical* minimum and maximum values of X and Y, which are values not necessarily observed in the dataset. For example, the minima and maxima of X and Y could be based on the minima and maxima of their measurement scales, the minima and maxima that were observed in earlier empirical studies, or the minima and maxima that are theoretically possible. Normally the empirical scope is used, as I do in this book. With the theoretical scope the effect size (see below) is usually larger than the effect size with the empirical scope. Therefore, you might be reluctant to use the theoretical scope because of the risk of overestimating the effect size.

The choice of using the empirical or theoretical scope determines the number of levels that the X and Y variables have for the analysis. For instance, a variable may have three theoretical levels (Low, Medium, High) but it could be that only two levels are observed (e.g. Low and Medium). The scope is calculated from the number of levels of X and Y. In general, when X has q theoretical or empirically observed levels, and

Y has r theoretical or empirically observed levels, the size of the contingency table is q x r cells and the scope (S) can be calculated as follows:

$$S = (q \times r) - q - r + 1 \text{ (Eq. 1)}$$

where S is the scope, q is the number of levels of X, and r is the number of levels of Y, assuming an interval scale. Thus, you can calculate the scope by counting the total number of cells from the contingency table minus the number of cells of a column, minus the number of cells of a row, plus 1.

In the example the size of the contingency table is $q \times r = 2 \times 2 = 4$; the number of X-levels q = 2, and the number of Y-levels r = 2. Thus, the scope is $4 - 2 - 2 + 1 = 1$.

Ceiling zone The size of the 'empty' zone in the corner expected to be empty is calculated by counting the number of 'empty' cells that make up the ceiling zone.

In the example the size of the ceiling zone (C) is 1.

Effect size The effect size (*d*) is the size of the ceiling zone in comparison to the scope and is calculated by dividing the ceiling zone by the scope:

$$d = C/S \text{ (Eq. 2)}$$

where *d* is the effect size, C is the ceiling zone, and S is the scope. The effect size can have values between 0, which corresponds to X having no necessity effect on Y, to 1, which corresponds to X having a maximum necessity effect on Y. If both variables are dichotomous, the effect size can be only 0 or 1.

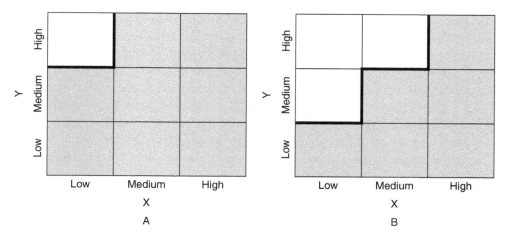

Figure 4.3   The effect size for a trichotomous necessary condition.
A: Effect size = 0.25. B: Effect size = 0.75.

If both variables are trichotomous, the scope is 4, and the ceiling zone can be zero, one, two, three, or four cells, which corresponds to effect sizes of 0, 0.25, 0.5, 0.75

and 1, respectively. For example, in the trichotomous case of Figure 4.3A one cell is empty and thus the effect size is 1/4 = 0.25, and in Figure 4B three cells are empty and thus the effect size is 3/4 = 0.75.

In the example regarding the necessity of individualism for a country's innovation, the effect size is $d = 1/1 = 1$.

c-accuracy The ceiling accuracy is the number of cases that are not in the ceiling zone, divided by the total number of cases, multiplied by 100%. If no cases are in the ceiling zone, the *c*-accuracy is 100%. If 1 out of 20 cases were in the ceiling zone, the *c*-accuracy is 19/20 x 100% = 95%.

In the example the *c*-accuracy is 100% because the ceiling zone is empty.

Step 5: Evaluate the NCA parameters

In this step the effect size and *c*-accuracy are evaluated and interpreted.

Effect size The effect size represents the substantive significance of the necessity effect of X for Y. The substantive significance is the meaningfulness of the effect size from a practical perspective. With a small effect size, for example when only one of the upper left cells in the trichotomous case is empty (see Figure 4.3A), the effect size is 0.25 and X constrains Y only for the Low value of X, and Y is constrained by X for only a High value of Y. With a larger effect size, for example when three upper left cells in the trichotomous case are empty (see Figure 4.3B), the effect size is 0.75 and X constrains Y for a larger range of X values (Low and Medium), and Y is constrained by X for a larger range of Y values (Medium and High).

It depends on the context whether or not an effect size has much substantive significance. From a practical perspective, a small effect size can be relatively important, and a large effect size can be relatively unimportant. This depends for example on how simple or complex it is to realise the required value of X in the range that X is necessary. The practical relevance can also depend on how common or rare X or Y is in the necessary range of X and Y values. For example, when a Low level of X in Figure 4.3A is rare and at least a Medium level of X is usually present, it may be relatively easy to implement the required level of the necessary condition.

In the example of the necessity of a country's individualism for innovation performance, the necessity effect size is 1 and is maximum. This is a large necessary condition because X constrains Y over the entire range of X and Y values (Low and High). It is not possible to have high innovation performance with low individualism, and a low level of X may be considered not rare (2 out of 7 cases).

c-accuracy The *c*-accuracy can be evaluated by comparing it with a benchmark value of for example 95%. There is no strict rule on what percentage of accuracy is acceptable. A required accuracy of 95% is arbitrary and is obtained when not more than 1 out of the 20 cases is in the empty space. Hence, no exception is accepted in small N research with less than 20 cases.

In the example of the necessity of a country's individualism for innovation performance, the c-accuracy is at the maximum of 100%. There are no outliers. Outliers would not be acceptable given the small number of cases.

Step 6: Formulate the conclusion

Based on the analyses in the previous steps, in Step 6 you need to draw a conclusion about the necessary condition hypothesis. You may conclude that the necessary condition hypothesis should be rejected because cases are present in the space that was expected to be empty. You can base this conclusion on a deterministic or probabilistic view about necessity. You may also conclude that the space that was expected to be empty is indeed (almost) empty and that the necessary condition hypothesis is not rejected and may be considered as supported in the present study. There are then two ways to formulate the necessary condition. The first formulation is a formulation 'in kind': 'X is necessary for Y'. This general formulation is based on the finding that the effect size $d > 0$. This is the least informative formulation of a necessary condition. Additionally, it is possible to formulate the necessary condition 'in degree'. In this formulation a row in the contingency table with a given level of Y is selected, and the level of X that is necessary for this Y is formulated: 'level X is necessary for level Y'. Hence, the 'in degree' formulation of the necessary condition gives more detail than the 'in kind' formulation.

In the example, the necessary condition 'in kind' is 'Individualism is necessary for Innovation performance', and the necessary condition 'in degree' is 'high Individualism is necessary for high Innovation performance'.

I have shown that the contingency approach for NCA's data analysis is rather simple. The analysis is based on visual inspection of the data, and with a few simple calculations you can quantify the effect size. The contingency approach is useful when the variable scores have a small number of levels, for example in small N studies. When the scores can be expressed as numbers, all analyses can *also* be done with the scatter plot approach and the NCA software using the CE-FDH ceiling line that I discuss in the next section. The scatter plot approach is particularly useful when the variable scores have a large number of levels, for example in large N studies.

DATA ANALYSIS WITH THE SCATTER PLOT APPROACH

The 'scatter plot approach' has the same six steps as the contingency approach, but the content of the steps can be different

- Step 1: Make the scatter plot.
- Step 2: Identify the empty space.

- Step 3: Draw the ceiling line.
- Step 4: Quantify the NCA parameters.
- Step 5: Evaluate the NCA parameters.
- Step 6: Formulate the conclusion.

This approach requires more advanced mathematical and statistical procedures compared to the 'contingency table approach'. Hence, it uses the NCA software for performing the analysis. The NCA software is a free package in R. R is an open source programming language that is commonly used for data analysis. Even if you do not know R, I suggest that you start getting familiar with it as it is becoming one of the main tools in research for statistical analysis and data visualisation. Without knowledge of R and NCA you can do your first quantitative NCA data analysis within 30 minutes. In this section I shall guide you through this process.

Before you can use the NCA software you must do three things:

1. Install R and RStudio on your computer.
2. Install the NCA R package on your computer.
3. Import your dataset into R.

Appendix 2 gives instructions on how to do this, and for more details and advice you can consult the Quick Start Guide which can be found online (Dul, 2018) and on the NCA website (www.erim.nl/nca).

```
> library("NCA") #loads the NCA package
> data(nca.example) #loads the nca.example dataset
> data<-nca.example #renames the nca.example dataset into 'data'
> data<-data[-c(14,22,26),]#deletes the 3 non-Western countries from dataset
> data #prints the data in the console window
             Individualism Risk taking Innovation performance
Australia             90          84                    50.9
Austria               55          65                    52.4
Belgium               75          41                    75.1
Canada                80          87                    81.4
Czech Rep             58          61                    14.5
Denmark               74         112                   116.3
Finland               63          76                   173.1
France                71          49                    77.6
Germany               67          70                   109.5
Greece                35          23                    12.0
Hungary               80          53                     5.4
Ireland               70         100                    62.3
Italy                 76          60                    19.7
Mexico                30          53                     1.2
Netherlands           80          82                    68.7
New Zealand           79          86                    14.9
Norway                69          85                    75.1
Poland                60          42                     3.5
Portugal              27          31                    11.1
Slovak Rep            52          84                     3.5
Spain                 51          49                    17.3
Sweden                71         106                   184.9
Switzerland           68          77                   149.7
UK                    89         100                    79.4
USA                   91          89                   214.4
```

Figure 4.4 Output from the NCA software in R. The first five lines are instructions for loading the NCA package, for loading and renaming the nca.example dataset, for deleting non-Western countries from the dataset, and for displaying the dataset in the console window of R.

Figure 4.4 shows how you can work with the NCA software after you have installed R. The first line is the instruction after the '>' prompt to load the NCA package, which must be done every time that you start a new R session. Normally you will type an instruction in the 'script window' of RStudio and click the Run button to execute the instruction. After running an instruction, R displays the instruction in the 'console window' after the prompt. In this book instructions in R are printed in the Courier font. The first instruction is `library(NCA)` which loads the NCA R package (after it has been installed on your computer; see Appendix 2). After this instruction some information about NCA is displayed in the console (not shown in Figure 4.4) and you are ready to work with NCA. Note that in Figure 4.4 I also included a # symbol after the instruction and added some explanatory text. R ignores text after this symbol, which is useful for making comments and annotating your script. The second instruction in Figure 4.4 is `data(nca.example)`. This loads the example dataset called nca.example that is included in the NCA package. This is the same example as in Figure 4.1 except that it includes some non-Western countries. Appendix 2 shows how you can load your own dataset. The third instruction is `data <- nca.example`, which renames the dataset into 'data'. The combination of symbols '<' and '–' is the 'assignment operator' of R that connects two objects, in this case 'data' and the data file. After this instruction your data are a 'data object' known as 'data'. The fourth instruction deletes the three non-Western countries from the dataset. The fifth instruction is `data` or `print(data)`. This just displays the data in the console window. The data in Figure 4.4 correspond to the data in Figure 4.1B. However, Figure 4.4 also includes the variable Risk taking. The scores on Risk taking were obtained from Hofstede (1980) by inverting uncertainty avoidance scores. Having a second variable allows for testing another necessary condition hypothesis: a country's culture of risk-taking is necessary for a country's innovation performance.

NCA is fundamentally a bivariate analysis: only two variables are analysed at a time (one X and one Y). When more variables are potential necessary conditions (like Individualism and Risk taking in the nca.example), the analysis is done for these conditions separately. Single bivariate analyses are possible because a necessary condition operates in isolation from the rest of the causal structure. Thus, with several potential necessary conditions NCA employs multiple bivariate analyses, rather than a multi-variate analysis. This is possible because the necessity of X1 on Y does not depend on the necessity of X2 on Y. I use the NCA software and the nca.example to illustrate the scatter plot approach.

Step 1: Make the scatter plot

A scatter plot of X and Y is a graph in which the X-axis is 'horizontal' and the Y axis is 'vertical', and values increase 'to the right' and 'upward'. Each case has a certain combination of X and Y values and is displayed in the scatter plot as a dot.

Figures 2.4I and 2.5 are examples of scatter plots, but without the specification of the cases in the dark area.

The reason for making a scatter plot is that you can compare the observed pattern of the data in the scatter plot, with the expected pattern when X is necessary for Y. The expected pattern depends on how you define your necessary condition hypothesis. If you define your hypothesis as 'a high level of X is necessary for a high level of Y', you could expect a scatter plot that looks like the one in Figure 2.5A with an empty space in the upper left corner.

Figure 4.5 shows the scatter plots of the example as produced by the NCA software. You can use the main instruction `nca_analysis` for making the scatter plot and the NCA calculations. The instruction `nca_output` can be used for producing the output. In the instruction `nca_analysis(data,x,y)`, data is the dataset, x is variable name or column number corresponding to the presumed necessary condition(s), and y is the name or column number corresponding to the outcome. Hence, for nca.example the instructions for the calculations are: `model<-nca_ana lysis(data,c("Individualism", "Risk taking"),"Innovation performance")`, or `model<-nca_analysis(data,c(1,2),3)`, where the two conditions are analysed separately but at the same time (the operator 'c' combines the column numbers). You can give the analysis a name, for example 'model'. For getting output for this analysis you can use the instruction `nca_output`. With the instruction `nca_output (model, plots=T)` (T means TRUE) the two scatter plots as shown in Figure 4.5 are displayed in the 'plot' window of RStudio.

Step 2: Identify the empty space

In the second step you need to identify by visual inspection of the scatter plot if an empty space exists in the corner that you expected to be empty given your necessary condition hypothesis. Assuming that a high level of X is necessary for a high level of Y, the expected empty space is in the upper left corner. As with the contingency table approach, this visual inspection can encounter three situations. First, *the expected empty space is empty*. The condition may be necessary because it is not possible to have a high level of the outcome without a high level of the condition. You can continue with Step 3. Second, *the expected empty space is clearly not empty*. There are many cases present in the area that you expected to be empty, and the condition is not necessary because it is possible to have the outcome without the condition. You continue the analysis with Step 6. Third, *the empty space is almost empty*. For example, one case may be present in the very upper left corner (observation with X = Xmin and Y = Ymax) such that there is no empty space, or one case is present in the otherwise empty space and far away from other cases. Similarly, as in the contingency table approach (Step 2 in the section 'Data analysis with the contingency

```
> model<-nca_analysis(data,c("Individualism", "Risk taking"),"Innovation performance
> nca_output(model, plots = T) # XY scatterplots
```

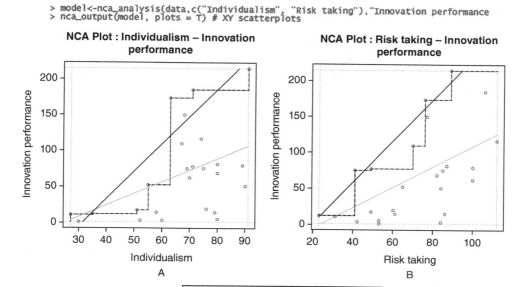

Figure 4.5 Output from the NCA software in R. The first line of code is the core instruction for conducting NCA and the second line produces the scatter plots.

A: scatter plot for testing the hypothesis that a country's individualism is necessary for a country's innovation. B: scatter plot for testing the hypothesis that a country's risk taking is necessary for a country's innovation. The expected empty spaces in the upper left corner are empty. The step function is the Ceiling Envelopment - Free Disposal Hull (CE-FDH) ceiling line. The straight ceiling line is the Ceiling Regression - Free Disposal Hull (CR-FDH) ceiling line. The line through the middle of the data is the Ordinary Least Squares (OLS) regression line, for reference. The horizontal and vertical dashed lines on the sides of the plot mark the empirical scope, hence the minimum and maximum observed values for X and Y.

table approach' p. 47), you can evaluate outliers in three ways. First, the outlier can be due to measurement error or sample error and may be removed from the analysis. Second, you can adopt a *probabilistic* view on necessity (chapter 'Philosophical Assumptions and Logic of NCA', section 'Deterministic and probabilistic views on necessity', p.17). Here you will need to consider outliers as exceptions or anomalies for unknown reasons and accept a relatively small number of outliers in the 'empty' space. You can then continue the analysis with Step 3, ignoring the outliers. Third, if you have a *deterministic* view on necessity (Chapter 'Philosophical Assumptions and Logic of NCA', section 'Deterministic and probabilistic views on necessity') you must consider the presence of even one case in the 'empty' space as the reason for rejecting the hypothesis. You would then continue the analysis with Step 6. The space that is empty or 'almost empty' is called the *ceiling zone*.

Step 3: Draw the ceiling line

The next step in NCA's scatter plot approach is to draw the ceiling line. A ceiling line is a line that separates the space without cases from the rest of the space. A good ceiling line should have a minimum number of cases above it and a maximum number of cases below it. Furthermore, a good ceiling line should follow the shape of the border, and hence should use the cases that are around the border rather than the cases far below it. Figure 4.5 shows three lines. Clearly, the OLS regression line through the middle of the cases (which is the average effect line) is not a good candidate for the ceiling line. The OLS line has too many observations above it, and too few cases below it, and is thus overestimating the size of the empty space. This seems obvious, but it is a main argument against the use of average effect analyses such as OLS regression or structural equation modelling for testing necessary conditions. Only for reference, the OLS line through the middle of the cases is shown in NCA plots as representing the *average* Y for a given value of X. In contrast, a ceiling line on top of the cases represents the *maximum* Y for a given value of X.

NCA offers two default ceiling lines: Ceiling Envelopment – Free Disposal Hull (CE-FDH) and Ceiling Regression – Free Disposal Hull (CR-FDH). CE-FDH is based on the Free Disposal Hull (FDH) frontier line that is used in operations research (Tulkens, 1993). It is a non-decreasing step-wise linear line ('step function') that can be used as the ceiling line when X or Y are discrete or when the pattern of points near the border is irregular. The CE-FDH ceiling line does not allow points above the line and produces the largest really empty space with a non-decreasing (piecewise) straight ceiling line. The line is drawn as follows (see the step function in Figure 4.5). Start at the origin of the scatter plot (where X = Xmin and Y = Ymin) and move vertically upward to the case with the highest Y for X = Xmin. Move horizontally to the right until a case is reached that is on or vertically above this horizontal line. Move vertically upward until the observation with the highest Y. Repeat the last two steps until the horizontal line reaches X = Xmax. The points of the upper left corners of the CE-FDH line are called the 'peers'.

The ceiling line CR-FDH (Ceiling Regression – Free Disposal Hull) is a straight trend line through the peers of the CE-FDH line. This line is a trend line through CE-FDH using simple linear regression by minimising the squared vertical distances of the line to the peers. The CR-FDH ceiling line can be used when X and Y are continuous or discrete with many levels, and when the pattern of points near the border is approximately linear. Another reason to select this line is when it is assumed that the 'true' ceiling line in the population is a straight line. The CR-FDH line has some points above it because CR-FDH is a trend line through the peers of CE-FDH. In Figure 4.5A five points are above the CR-FDH line, and in Figure 4.5B four points are above it.

Other ceiling lines can be selected with the NCA software as well. For example, the Ceiling Envelopment - Varying Return to Scale (CE-VRS) ceiling technique could be used when the ceiling line should reflect that the increase of maximum Y with increasing X diminishes with increasing X. The CE-VRS line is a concave piecewise linear ceiling line. The corresponding instruction is nca_analysis(data,c(1,2),3, ceilings = "ce_vrs"). In the future other lines (e.g. polynomial functions with improved statistical properties) may be introduced. Currently the CE-FDH and CR-FDH ceiling lines serve most purposes of NCA. Research can use one of the two default ceiling lines or can perform the analysis with both default ceiling lines, e.g. for testing the robustness by comparing the results.

Step 4: Quantify the NCA parameters

In this step the NCA parameters are calculated. The main parameter is the necessity effect size. In order to calculate this parameter, the scope and ceiling zone must be calculated first. The instructions nca_analysis and nca_output can be used for making the calculations, and producing the output. In Figure 4.6 the default ceiling lines CE-FDH and CR-FDH are selected and their NCA parameters are calculated. I only show results for the condition Individualism.

```
> model<-nca_analysis(data,1,3, ceilings = c("ce_fdh", "cr_fdh"))
> nca_output(model)

--------------------------------------------------------------
NCA Parameters : Individualism - Innovation performance
--------------------------------------------------------------

Number of observations    25
Scope                 13644.8
Xmin                     27.0
Xmax                     91.0
Ymin                      1.2
Ymax                    214.4

                      ce_fdh    cr_fdh
Ceiling zone        7869.600  6928.774
Effect size            0.577     0.508
# above                    0         5
c-accuracy              100%       80%
Fit                     100%     88.0%

Slope                             3.805
Intercept                      -118.621
Abs. ineff.          633.600   743.780
Rel. ineff.            4.644     5.451
Condition ineff.       0.000     5.451
Outcome ineff.         4.644     0.000
```

Figure 4.6   Output from the NCA software in R. The first line is the core instruction for conducting an NCA analysis with the two default ceiling lines and without the OLS regression line. The second line prints a summary of the NCA parameters in the 'console window' of R. Only the output for Individualism is shown.

Scope The first six lines of the printed output show general information about the data: the number of observations (cases), the scope (the area between the minimum and maximum values of X and Y), and the minima and maxima of X and Y. By default the scope refers to the empirical scope. There may be theoretical arguments that the true minimum value is lower than the observed value, and the true maximum value is higher than the observed value. Then, if desired, a theoretical scope can be selected by specifying the minimum and maximum values of X and Y, for example: `model<-nca_analysis(data,1,3,ceilings = c("ce_fdh", "cr_fdh"), scope=c(0, 120, 0, 240))`. For a discussion on the theoretical versus the empirical scope see the section 'Data analysis with the contingency table approach', Step 4 'Quantify the NCA parameters' under 'Scope' (p. 76).

Ceiling zone In the middle group of parameters first the ceiling zone is displayed. The ceiling zone is the zone above the ceiling line within the scope. Usually CR-FDH produces a smaller ceiling zone than CE-FDH.

Effect size The effect size is the Ceiling zone (C) divided by the scope (S), and has values between 0 and 1. For the CE-FDH ceiling line in the example, the effect size is $7869.6/13644.8 = 0.577$.

C-accuracy and fit The middle group also shows the number of observations (cases) above the ceiling and the ceiling line accuracy (*c*-accuracy), which is the percentage of cases that are on or below the ceiling line. In the example, the *c*-accuracy for CE-FDH is 100% (by definition), and the *c*-accuracy for CR-FDH is 80%. The fit score is the effect size of a selected ceiling line divided by the effect size of the CE-FDH ceiling line. By definition for CE-FDH the fit is 100%. For CR-FDH the fit in the example is 88%.

Ceiling slope and intercept In the last group of parameters the *slope* and *intercept* of the ceiling line are given if the ceiling line is a straight line, which is true for CR-FDH. The next four parameters are about '*necessity inefficiency*', offering a more advanced set of parameters that I discuss in Box 4.2.

Box 4.2   What is necessity inefficiency?

Necessity inefficiency is a more advanced NCA parameter. The effect size indicates to what extent the condition X constrains outcome Y. When both the full space and the empty space are triangular, hence the ceiling line corresponds to the diagonal of the scatter plot, any value of X constrains Y, and any value of Y is constrained by X. In most situations, however, only a part of the range of X constrains Y and only part of the range of Y is constrained by X. This happens, for example, when the empty space is triangular and the full space is pentagonal, as for example in Figure 2.5A. When the ceiling line intersects the horizontal line Y = Ymax, X does not constrain Y for values of X from this intersection point to the maximum value of X. For reaching Ymax it is necessary to have the X that corresponds to this intersection point. A higher value of X is not necessary for Y, hence in practice it could be inefficient to increase X beyond the intersection point.

This inefficient range of X multiplied by the maximum range if Y, and expressed as a percentage of the scope, is called 'condition inefficiency', i.e. the area of the scope where X does not constrain Y. Similarly, when the ceiling line intersects the vertical axis X = 0, Y is not constrained by X for values of Y from zero to the intersection point. Hence, in practice it would be inefficient to increase X for allowing Y in this range of Y. This inefficient range of Y multiplied by the maximum range of X, and expressed as a percentage of the scope, is called 'outcome inefficiency', i.e. the area of the scope where Y is not constrained by X. The total unconstrained area is called Absolute inefficiency, and this area as percentage of the scope is called the Relative inefficiency.

Step 5: Evaluate the NCA parameters

In this step the effect size is evaluated in two ways. To begin with the substantive significance of the effect size (d) is considered, and subsequently the statistical significance of the effect size (p). Afterwards the ceiling accuracy is evaluated, as well as the so called 'influential cases', including outliers.

Evaluation of substantive significance of the effect size

The effect size is a quantitative expression of the size of the constraint of X on Y. The effect size has values between 0 and 1 and represents the substantive significance of the necessity effect of X for Y. The higher the effect size, the larger the constraint that X puts on Y, and the more that Y is constrained by X. The substantial importance of the effect size depends on the context. An effect size may be important in one context but not in another. Therefore the researcher must give substantive reasons why an effect size is important in a given context. A small effect indicates that only a small range of X constrains Y, and/or only a small range of Y is constrained by X. But within this range, X is still necessary for Y. A small effect may be considered important or not depending on the context. For example, if a company wants to be the best performer among its competitors (Y is performance), a small necessity effect size where X is only necessary for the highest levels of Y will be considered as important. On the other hand, when a company wants to be just a good average performer but not an exceptionally good one, the small effect size may not be important when X does not constrain the desired level of performance. Therefore, it depends on the context whether or not an effect size can be considered as important. Information about the size of the effect, the inclination of the ceiling line, and 'condition inefficiency' and 'outcome inefficiency' (see Box 4.2) might be combined with the researcher's contextual knowledge to judge the importance of the effect size. For example, when Y is a desired outcome and the outcome in efficiency is large, the effect size may not be important if the highest outcome is not desired. But if the highest outcome is desired this effect size may be very important and the right level of the condition must be in place to allow that outcome. When an substantive evaluation of the effect size is not possible you may want to classify the effect size by using the general benchmark where $0 < d < 0.1$ is considered a 'small effect', $0.1 \leq d < 0.3$ a 'medium effect', $0.3 \leq d < 0.5$ a 'large effect', and $d \geq 0.5$ a 'very large effect'. This guideline is based on my experience with evaluating hundreds of scatter plots of discrete and continuous variables that could have meaningful empty spaces based on theoretical or practical argumentations. About half of the observed effect sizes (calculated with the empirical scope) were below 0.1, about 40% were between 0.1 and 0.3, and about 10% were between 0.3 and 0.5. Effect sizes above 0.5, which are possible with the CE-FDH ceiling line are rare. Several researchers have used the general threshold value of effect size $d = 0.1$ as the criterion to accept or reject a necessary condition hypothesis (e.g. Karwowski et al., 2016; Van der Valk et al., 2016; Luther et al., 2017; Knol et al., 2018).

In the example of a country's individualism and innovation performance the CE-FDH effect size is 0.577. According to the general benchmark, this effect size can be considered as 'very large'.

Evaluation of the statistical significance of the effect size

Evaluating the effect size based only on substantive importance may be risky. It is possible that an empty space in the scatter plot is the result of random chance of two unrelated variables and not the result of a necessity relationship between X and Y. This can be illustrated with the simulated scatter plot of two unrelated normally distributed random variables (Figure 4.7A). Figure 4.7A has empty spaces in all corners, including the upper left corner. The calculated effect sizes for the CE-FDH and CR-FDH ceiling lines are both 0.09, hence not zero. The two unrelated random variables in Figure 4.7B have a skewed distribution. The X variable is left skewed such that low X values are relatively rare and the Y variable is right skewed such that high Y values are relatively rare. These distributions of random variables produce an empty space in the upper left corner of the scatter plot that has no necessity meaning. The effect sizes for the CE-FDH and CR-FDH ceiling lines are 0.13 and 0.15, respectively. Notice that in both cases the *average* effect of X on Y is zero as correctly represented by the OLS regression line. However, the necessity effect is not zero and the researcher could erroneously conclude that X may be necessary for Y. Without applying a statistical test a researcher could draw invalid conclusions about a necessity relationship.

NCA's statistical test (see Box 4.3), like most significance tests, first assumes that X and Y are unrelated and that data of the sample are the result of a random process in the population: the 'null hypothesis' is true. NCA uses the observed sample for generating alternative samples where X and Y are unrelated such that the null hypothesis applies. This is done by reshuffling X and Y. This is repeated many times to obtain many samples called 'permutations' (e.g. 10,000) where a possible observed effect size is due to random chance because the null hypothesis is true. For each random sample the effect size is calculated, resulting in a distribution of random effect sizes when the null hypothesis holds. Now the effect size of the observed sample is compared with the random effect sizes. The *p* value is the probability that the effect size of the observed sample is equal to or larger than the effect sizes of the samples where X and Y are unrelated. If this probability is very small (e.g. $p < 0.05$) it is concluded that it is not plausible that the observed effect size is the result of a random process of unrelated variables: the null hypothesis is rejected. This is an indication that an alternative, including the necessary condition hypothesis may be true. Note that it is an inherent characteristic of any null hypothesis test that the null hypothesis of randomness is tested, not the alternative hypothesis. For accepting an empty space as representing a necessary condition three necessary but not sufficient conditions must be met: theorietical support, a large effect size (e.g., $d > 0.1$), and a small p-value ($P < 0.05$).

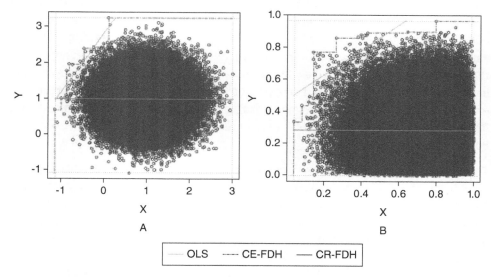

Figure 4.7 Scatter plots of two unrelated random variables X and Y showing 100,000 observations.

A: X and Y each have a normal distribution (mean = 1, SD = 0.5). B: X and Y each have a skewed beta distribution (X: first shape parameter = 5, second shape parameter = 2; Y: first shape parameter = 2, second shape parameter = 5). The empty space in the upper left corner of both plots got there by chance and cannot be interpreted as necessity.

Applying NCA's statistical test to the random data of Figure 4.7 reveals that the test can recognise that the empty spaces in the upper left corners are likely due to random chance of unrelated variables. For the situation with normal distributions of X and Y (see Figure 4.7A) the p value is 0.383, and for the situation with the skewed distributions of X and Y (see Figure 4.7B) the p value is 0.370. Hence, in both situations the observed effects are not rare ($p > 0.05$). There is no indication that the null hypothesis does not explain the data, hence the test correctly suggests that the null hypothesis should not be rejected. The NCA's statistical test helps prevent your drawing a false positive conclusion, i.e. concluding that X is necessary for Y whereas actually X and Y are unrelated.

The p value is much debated, much misunderstood, and much misused for statistical inference. NCA uses the p value to check the probability that the observed empty space is a random result of unrelated variables (see Box 4.3).

Box 4.3   What is the *p* value and how is it used in NCA?

According to Fisher (1925), statistical significance is the theoretical probability (*p* value) that the value of a test statistic that summarises the sample data (e.g. effect size) is equal to, or larger than, the observed value of this test statistic under the assumption that a null hypothesis is true. If the null hypothesis is true (i.e. there is no relationship between X and Y and thus no necessity effect), any observed sample effect would be due to random chance, and drawing repeated samples would result in a distribution of random effect sizes. If the effect size of the observed sample is relatively large, thus near the right tail of the distribution of random effects, the corresponding *p* value is relatively small: few random effects are larger. Fisher interpreted a small observed *p* value as either a rare result that happens only with probability *p* (or lower), or as an indication that the null hypothesis does not explain the data.

The *p* value concept is not very intuitive. It is therefore not surprising that many misinterpretations are around. For example, a high *p* value is not the probability that the null hypothesis is true, and a low *p* value is not the probability that the alternative hypothesis is true. Low *p* values provide only indirect evidence for the hypothesis of interest and may help to avoid a Type I error: rejecting a true null hypothesis.

In NCA we go back to the roots of the *p* value: testing the likelihood that the observed data were obtained just by chance of unrelated variables, hence testing whether the data fit the null hypothesis that the observed empty space in the upper left corner is due to random chance of unrelated variables. Since it is possible that two unrelated variables may produce an empty space in the upper left corner that has no necessity meaning, performing a statistical significance test is particularly important for NCA. If the test shows that randomness is not likely (e.g. $p < 0.05$), the researcher may conclude that randomness is still possible, though rare, because p is not zero or that alternative explanations exist for how the data were produced. One such alternative explanation is the hypothesis of interest: the observed empty space in the upper left corner may be caused by a necessity relationship between X and Y. NCA uses the p value as a randomness test to protect the researcher against Type I error and concluding that the empty space represents necessity, when it is actually a random occurrence.

NCA's significance test is a null hypothesis test that has the following parts (Dul et al., forthcoming):

1. Calculate the necessity effect size for the sample.
2. Formulate the null hypothesis that suggests that X and Y in the population are not related. Any effect size is a random effect.
3. Create a large set of random resamples (e.g. 10,000) using approximate permutation. In a permutation test the X and Y values that are observed in the sample are shuffled to create new resamples (same sample size) with 'cases' where X and Y are unrelated.
4. Calculate the effect size of all resamples. The set of effect sizes comprises an estimated distribution of effect size under the assumption that X and Y are not related.
5. Compare the effect size of the observed sample (see part 1) with the distribution of effect sizes of the random resamples. The fraction of random resamples for which the effect size is equal to, or greater than, the observed effect size (p value), informs us about the statistical (in)compatibility of the data with the null hypothesis.

A researcher who applies NCA may wish to use the p value for making conclusions about the support for the hypothesis that X is necessary for Y. However, a low p value does not by itself make a necessary condition plausible. There must also be theoretical support for it, in particular for observational studies, and the effect size must be meaningful. Even then the result may be due to chance. Only after replications show similar results, can the researcher become confident that the necessary condition is 'true'. This careful reasoning about a 'true' theoretical claim holds for any data analysis approach that uses the p value as one of the decision criteria. NCA's statistical test can be performed with the NCA software.

NCA's statistical test for the example is shown in Figure 4.8.

```
> model<-nca_analysis(data,1:2,3,test.rep = 10000) # 10000 permutations
Done test for Individualism
Done test for Risk taking
> model # print main results

--------------------------------------------------------------------------
Effect size(s):
            ce_fdh p      cr_fdh p
Individualism 0.577  0.003 0.508  0.003
Risk taking   0.464  0.008 0.384  0.014
--------------------------------------------------------------------------

> nca_output(model, test = T) #print effect size distribution
```

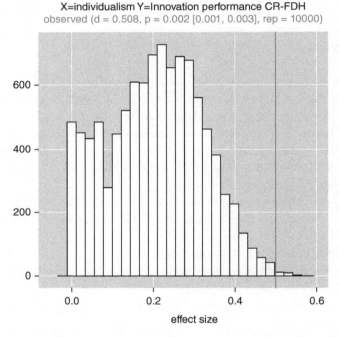

X=individualism Y=Innovation performance CR-FDH
observed (d = 0.508, p = 0.002 [0.001, 0.003], rep = 10000)

effect size

Figure 4.8 Output from the statistical test with the NCA software in R. The first line is the core instruction for conducting the test. The output is a plot with effect size on the horizontal axis and number of permutations (with random effect sizes) on the vertical axis. The observed effect size (vertical line) can be compared with the distribution of random effect sizes. The observed effect size is larger than the majority of random effect sizes, suggesting no support for the null hypothesis.

In nca_analysis the argument `test.rep = 10000` means that 10,000 resamples are selected to be drawn from all permutations, which is the recommended number of resamples to estimate the *p* value. With the instruction `model` or `print(model))` a summary of effect sizes and the corresponding *p* values is displayed. In `nca_output` instruction `test = T` (T = TRUE) means that the output displays the plot with the distribution of the effect sizes of the resamples and the values of the observed sample. Only the output for CR-FDH effect sizes for Individualism is shown. On the top of this plot the estimated effect size and the estimated *p* value (with 95% confidence interval) are given. The confidence interval of the estimated *p* value becomes smaller when more resamples are drawn (e.g. 100,000). It turns out that the *p* values for Individualism and Risk taking are well below 0.05. Thus, the probability that the observed effect size is due to random chance of unrelated variables is relatively small, which makes the hypothesis that Individualism and Risk taking are necessary for Innovation performance more plausible.

Evaluation of accuracy and influential cases

c-accuracy The relatively low *c*-accuracy and fit for CR-FDH is due to the non-regular pattern of the observations near the ceiling. Hence, in this example CE-FDH may be a better choice for the ceiling line than CR-FDH. The ceiling accuracy of the CE-FDH line is by definition 100%.

Influential cases Influential cases are cases that have a large influence on the effect size when deleted. Cases that are used to draw the ceiling line can be influential cases and cases below the ceiling line can be non-influential cases. The cases that make up the ceiling line are called 'peers'. The peers of a ceiling line can be found by the instruction `nca(data,c(1,2),3)$peers or model$peers`. This instruction returns the case identifiers (case names or case numbers) and XY coordinates of the peers. Also the minimum or maximum values of X and Y can be influencial cases as they determine the scope and thus the effect size. The influential cases can be identified for two reasons. The influential cases can be checked for measurement error (are the scores correct?) or sample error (does the case belong to the intended theoretical domain or population?). Measurement error or sample error of these cases can have a large effect on the result. Further, influential cases and other cases around the ceiling line have relatively high Y for low X. If X is an effort, and Y is a desired outcome, these cases may be considered as 'best cases' that are able to reach a relatively high level of Y with a relatively low level of X. Hence, cases near the ceiling line might be a benchmark for cases below the ceiling. For example, countries around the ceiling line achieve a higher level of innovation performance for a given level of individualism than countries below the ceiling line. These benchmark countries perform better than other countries with similar levels of individualism, due to other factors than the necessary condition. Likewise, benchmark countries near the ceiling obtain a certain level of innovation performance with less individualism than countries below the ceiling line.

Step 6: Formulate the conclusion

In Step 2 you may have concluded by visual inspection that the upper left corner of the scatter plot is clearly not empty, and that this is not caused by outliers due to measurement or sample error. Hence, you would conclude that the necessary condition hypothesis is rejected. However, if you were to conclude that the upper left corner is (almost) empty, the effect size as calculated and evaluated in Steps 4 and 5 is considered by checking if the following three necessary conditions for a necessary condition have been met:

1. There is theoretical support for the necessary condition as expressed by the hypothesis.
2. The effect size (*d*) is larger than a selected threshold value (e.g. 0.1): substantive significance.
3. The *p* value of the effect size is smaller than a selected threshold value (e.g. 0.05): the effect size is not due to random chance by unrelated variables: statistical significance.

If one of these conditions is not met, you cannot conclude that X is necessary for Y and reject the hypothesis. For example, if in Step 5 you have observed that the empty space was too small and below the effect size threshold that you have set, you would reject the hypothesis. It is also possible that the effect size was large enough compared to the threshold, but that the *p* value was too large. The observed effect size may be the result of random chance of unrelated variables and not the result of necessity. Also, you would then conclude that the necessary condition hypothesis has been rejected.

When the three criteria all apply, you may decide that your necessary condition hypothesis is supported, although you can never be sure. You can then formulate the necessary condition in kind that 'X is necessary for Y'. Additionally, it is possible to formulate the necessary condition 'in degree' by using the bottleneck table. The bottleneck table is the tabular representation of the ceiling line. In this formulation 'level X is necessary for level Y'. Hence, the 'in degree' formulation of the necessary condition gives more detail than the 'in kind' formulation. When the ceiling line is a straight line (CR-FDH) its details can be expressed by the slope and the intercept. The slope and the intercept can be obtained with the instruction `nca_output (model)`.

In the example of individualism and innovation performance, the effect sizes are well above the threshold value of 0.1, and the *p* value is well below the threshold value of 0.05. Hence, the necessary condition hypothesis is not rejected and thus could be considered as being supported. The necessary conditions 'in kind' are then formulated as 'Individualism is necessary for Innovation' and 'Risk taking is necessary for Innovation'. The necessary conditions 'in degree' are 'level X_{ci} of Individualism is necessary for level Y_c of Innovation' and 'level X_{cr} of Risk taking is necessary for level Y_c of Innovation'. Figure 4.9 shows the bottleneck table for the CE-FDH lines of these two necessary conditions.

```
> model<-nca_analysis(data,c(1,2),3, ceilings = "ce_fdh")
> nca_output(model, summaries=F, bottlenecks = T) #print bottleneck table
--------------------------------------------------------------------
Bottleneck CE-FDH (cutoff = 0)
Y Innovation performance (percentage.range)
1 Individualism           (percentage.range)
2 Risk taking             (percentage.range)
--------------------------------------------------------------------
Y          1     2
0          NN    NN
10         43.8  20.2
20         43.8  20.2
30         56.2  20.2
40         56.2  52.8
50         56.2  52.8
60         56.2  59.6
70         56.2  59.6
80         56.2  59.6
90         100.0 74.2
100        100.0 74.2
```

Figure 4.9 Output from the bottleneck table analysis of the NCA software in R. The first line is the core instruction for conducting the NCA with the Ceiling Envelopment - Free Disposal Hull ceiling line. The second line displays the bottleneck table for this line. The values of X and Y are expressed in percentage of range in which 0 corresponds to the lowest observed value, and 100 to the highest observed value. NN means 'not necessary'.

The first column is the outcome Y (Innovation performance) usually expressed as a percentage of the range of Y, hence 0 represents the minimum value of Y and 100 represents the maximum value of Y. The next columns are the conditions (1 = Individualism; 2 = Risk taking). These variables are expressed as percentages of their ranges as well. The bottleneck table can be read as follows: for a given value of outcome Y, the table shows the necessary levels (minimum required levels) of the conditions. For example, when an outcome level of Y is below 10%, none of the two conditions is necessary to achieve that outcome (NN = not necessary). However, when the desired Y is between 10 and 20%, Individualism must be 43.8% and Risk taking 20.2%. For a level of Innovation performance between 40 and 80%, both conditions must be 50-60%. An Innovation performance level above 80% needs 100% Individualism and 74.2% Risk taking. For assisting the interpretation, performance the X and Y values can also be expressed as their actual values or as percentiles by using for the arguments `bottleneck.x` and `bottleneck.y` with values 'actual' or 'percentile', respectively.

I have shown that also the scatter plot approach for NCA's data analysis is relatively simple. The analysis can be quickly done with the NCA software. The scatter plot approach can be used for any NCA data analysis with numerical scores.

SUMMARY

This chapter showed NCA's data analysis approach for testing a necessary condition hypothesis with empirical data. The analysis is a (multiple) bivariate analysis, hence one condition is analysed at a time, and this analysis can be repeated for all conditions. In Step 1 you display combinations of X values and Y values that are observed in cases in an XY contingency table or an XY scatter plot. The contingency table approach allows a qualitative data analysis by visual inspection, e.g. in a small N study. The scatter plot approach allows for a quantitative data analysis with the NCA software, for example in a large N study. In Step 2 you identify whether there is an empty space without cases in the corner of the contingency table or the scatter plot that is the expected corner to be empty, given the hypothesis. In Step 3 you draw a ceiling line to separate the empty cells from the other cells of the contingency table or scatter plot. In Step 4 you determine the NCA parameter effect size. In the contingency table approach you can do this by counting the cells of the contingency table, and in the scatter plot approach you can use the NCA R software package. In Step 5 you evaluate the necessity effect size regarding its substantive and statistical significance. Finally, in Step 6 you draw a conclusion about the hypothesis. If the hypothesis is supported, you can formulate a necessary condition 'in kind' or a necessary condition 'in degree'.

5

NCA EXAMPLES

INTRODUCTION

In this chapter I present six examples of studies that apply NCA. The first example is a Master's thesis project that illustrates how NCA can be applied with the contingency table approach using qualitative data analysis by visual inspection. The second example is a re-analysis of existing data from a published article that illustrates how NCA can be applied with the scatter plot approach using a quantitative data analysis with the NCA software. I present both examples according to the stages of conducting NCA mentioned in Chapter 1 (see Figure 1.1): I discuss how the necessity condition hypothesis is formulated (Stage 1); how the data were collected (Stage 2); and how the data were analysed (Step 3). I will not discuss Stage 4 about reporting the results. In Appendix 3 I present general guidelines for writing up an NCA study.

The next set of examples are four published articles from different business and management fields: Operations Management, Entrepreneurship, Strategy, and Innovation. In these articles NCA is used as the main logic and data analysis methodology. I will discuss these four published articles by using the checklist in Figure 5.1. This checklist can be used for evaluating published articles that use NCA, as well as for writing your own publication with NCA.

The checklist consists of three parts: introduction, methods, and results. The *Intro* part includes the article's research question and contribution regarding necessity logic and the formulated necessary condition hypotheses. A contribution can be theoretical, practical or methodological, or a combination. Information about contributions and hypotheses is usually found in the 'Introduction', 'Theory' and 'Discussion' sections of an article.

The *Methods* part of the checklist is about the article's methods for collecting and analysing data. Methods for data collection refer to the research strategy, the selection or sampling of cases and the measurement of variables. The resulting dataset is the starting point for the data analysis with NCA. Methods for data analysis include drawing the ceiling line, calculating the effect size, and performing NCA's statistical test. Information about methods is usually found in the 'Methods' and 'Results' sections of an article.

The *Results* part of the checklist is about the reporting of the article's NCA results. This includes the presentation of the XY contingency table or scatter plot, the reporting of NCA parameters like effect size and ceiling accuracy, the substantive and statistical evaluation of the effect size, and a conclusion about the hypothesis test. The bottleneck table can be presented for formulating the necessary condition in degree. Information about results is usually found in the 'Results' section of an article.

			NCA topic
Intro	1		Formulation of intended contribution with necessity logic
	2		Formulation of theoretical necessity statement: hypothesis
Methods	3	Data	Specification of research strategy
	4		Specification of case selection/sampling
	5		Specification of measurement of all variables
	6	Data analysis	Specification of selected ceiling line
	7		Specification of effect size threshold
	8		Specification of statistical significance threshold
Results	9		Presentation of contingency table or scatter plot
	10		Report of NCA parameters (effect size, ceiling-accuracy)
	11		Substantive evaluation of effect size (*d*)
	12		Statistical evaluation of effect size (*p* value)
	13		Result of hypothesis test
	14		Presentation of bottleneck table

Figure 5.1   Checklist for a publication that uses NCA

EXAMPLE OF NCA WITH THE CONTINGENCY TABLE APPROACH

This example is about organisations that want to respond to the challenge of prolonged sitting by implementing physical activity programmes for their employees. What is necessary to successfully maintain such programmes after their implementation? This small N study (nine organisations), with dichotomous variables scores, was the topic of a Master's thesis research project, 'Necessary conditions for maintaining physical activity interventions' (Guiking, 2009). I first present how the necessary conditions were formulated (Stage 1), then how the data were collected (Stage 2), and finally how the data were analysed with the six steps of NCA's contingency table approach by visual inspection (Stage 3).

Stage 1: Formulation of the necessary condition hypothesis

The goal of this research is to contribute to the success of physical activity programmes in organisations. The general research question is 'Which factors contribute to successful maintenance of physical activity programmes?' This general research question is practically relevant, because the factors can be influenced by the organisation and the outcome is desired. The research focused on necessity logic. The specific research question is 'Which factors are *necessary* for successful maintenance of physical activity programmes?' To answer this research question, the researcher first categorised possible factors in the categories 'individual', 'organisational', and 'environmental'. She then identified from the literature and other sources an initial list of 25 potential necessary conditions. From this list she selected nine potential necessary conditions for the study based on her personal interests and feasibility for measurement. Based on this selection the following eight necessary condition hypotheses were formulated for testing:

- H1: The management perception that the programme is advantageous is necessary for successful maintenance of the physical activity programme (PRA = Perceived relative advantage).
- H2: The stimulation by management of employees to participate in the programme is necessary for successful maintenance of the physical activity programme (MC = Management commitment).
- H3: The presence of essential knowledge about the programme in the organisation is necessary for successful maintenance of the physical activity programme (K = Knowledge of intervention).
- H4: The presence of a programme champion in the organisation is necessary for successful maintenance of the physical activity programme (PC = Programme champion).
- H5: Sufficient (financial) resources are necessary for successful maintenance of the physical activity programme (FR = Financial resources).
- H6: The management perception that employees are committed to the programme is necessary for successful maintenance of the physical activity programme (IC = Individual commitment).
- H7: The possibility to experiment with the programme is necessary for successful maintenance of the physical activity programme (T = Triability).
- H8: The justifiability of costs of the programme is necessary for successful maintenance of the physical activity programme (C = Costs).

The focal unit of these hypotheses is an 'organisation's physical activity programme'. The theoretical domain where the hypothesis is supposed to hold is broad and might be 'all large organisations in the world with a physical activity programme'.

Stage 2: Collect data

The research strategy was a small N observational study. The researcher used purposive sampling and selected only successful cases. Success is defined as a physical activity programme that was continued after an initial period of funding or testing. The researcher selected cases from a population of Dutch organisations with a physical activity programme by using her personal network and the networks of selected organisations. The resulting convenience sample consisted of nine successful cases. Based on knowledge from informants in each organisation, who were managers and employees, the researcher verified that all selected cases were successful. For each case the eight independent variables (conditions) were measured as follows. First, the theoretical concept was precisely defined. Second, one or more dimensions of the concept were identified. Third, statements about the dimensions of the concept were formulated, to be rated on a five-point Likert scale or on a two-point yes/no scale by informants or respondents using questionnaires. Informants are persons who give information about something outside themselves, and respondents are persons who give information about themselves, e.g. opinions. Fourth, the researcher identified who were the best informants and respondents to rate the statements (employee, management, personnel involved in the programme). Sixth, the five-point scales were dichotomised (absent/present) by defining and justifying that a condition with a score of at least 3 is considered to be 'present'. The researcher visited all but one

	A	B	C	D	E	F	G	H	I	J
1	Organisation	PRA	MC	KI	PC	FR	IC	T	C	Success
2	1	Y	Y	Y	Y	Y	N	Y	Y	Y
3	2	Y	Y	Y	Y	Y	Y	Y	Y	Y
4	3	Y	Y	Y	N	Y	Y	Y	Y	Y
5	4	Y	Y	Y	N	Y	N	Y	Y	Y
6	5	Y	Y	Y	N	Y	Y	N	Y	Y
7	6	Y	Y	Y	N	Y	N	Y	Y	Y
8	7	Y	Y	Y	N	Y	N	Y	Y	Y
9	8	Y	Y	Y	N	Y	N	Y	Y	Y
10	9	Y	Y	Y	N	Y	Y	N	Y	Y

Figure 5.2 Dataset of nine organisations that successfully maintained physical activity programmes. First column: organisation identifier; last column: Success score. The other columns are qualitative variable scores of potential necessary conditions according to the eight formulated hypotheses (Y = yes, present; N = no, absent). PRA = Perceived relative advantage; MC = Management commitment; KI = Knowledge intervention; PC = Programme champion; FR = Financial resources; IC = Individual commitment; T = Triability; C = Costs. (Adapted from Guiking, 2009.)

organisation to understand the organisational context and to personally administer the questionnaires. The dataset for the nine cases with final scores for the eight independent variables and one dependent variable (success) is shown in Figure 5.2. The eight independent variables relate to the eight hypotheses: each independent variable is assumed to be a necessary condition.

Stage 3: Analyse data

Step 1: Make the contingency table

Figure 5.3 shows the contingency tables for testing two of the eight hypotheses, namely H2 about the necessity of Management commitment (MC), and H4 for the necessity of a Programme champion (PC). Each cell contains the number of cases with the observed combination of X and Y values. The total number of cases is nine. Notice the question mark in the cells for No 'Maintenance of programme'. The reason is that no cases were selected for these cells because only successful cases were selected, hence only the cells for Yes 'Maintenance of programme' could be filled. Selecting cases on the basis of the presence of the outcome is an efficient way to test dichotomous necessary conditions.

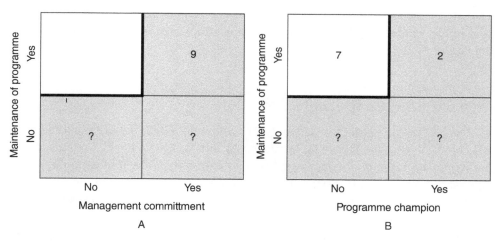

Figure 5.3 Contingency tables for testing two necessary condition hypotheses (H2 and H4) for maintenance of a physical activity programme in organisations.
A: Management commitment (MC), and B: Programme champion (PC).

Step 2: Identify the empty space

In Figure 5.3a an empty space is observed in the upper left corner that was expected to be empty, thus for Management commitment we continue with Step 3 of the data analysis approach. In Figure 5.3b the space in the upper left corner is not empty.

Seven out of nine cases (78%) are present in this cell: seven out of nine success-ful cases had no Programme champion. Thus, for Programme champion we continue with Step 6 of the data analysis approach.

Step 3: Draw the ceiling line

For Management commitment the ceiling line is drawn as a thick line in Figure 5.3A.

Step 4: Quantify the NCA parameters

For a dichotomous contingency table with an empty cell in the upper left corner the scope is 1, and the ceiling zone is 1. The effect size for Management commitment is thus 1. There are no cases in the empty space, hence the c-accuracy for Management commitment is 100%.

Step 5: Evaluate the NCA parameters

The effect size for Management commitment is maximum and obviously the researcher considered this as a meaningful effect size. Also the c-accuracy is maximum.

Step 6: Formulate the conclusion

In Step 2 it was found that for Management commitment (MC) the space in the upper left corner of the contingency table was empty with maximum effect size and ceiling accuracy. The researcher concluded that hypothesis H2, 'The stimulation by man-agement of employees to participate in the programme is necessary for successful maintenance of the physical activity programme', was supported (not falsified). The necessary condition can be formulated in kind as 'Management commitment is neces-sary for maintenance of the programme' or in degree as 'a high level of Management commitment is necessary for maintenance of the programme'.

In Step 2 it was found that for Programme champion (PC) the space in the upper left corner of the contingency table was clearly not empty. Based on this finding the researcher concluded that hypothesis H4, 'The presence of a pro-gramme champion in the organisation is necessary for successful maintenance of the physical activity programme', is rejected (falsified).

In general a rejection of a hypothesis might have several reasons (Chapter 'Basic Components of NCA, section 'Data analysis', p. 42). In this example the researcher first considers the possibility of measurement error (Guiking, 2009: 38-39):

The fact that in most organizations no PC appeared to be present can be the result of several causes. First of all, the question regarding the presence of a PC was often misunderstood or not understood at all. In some cases, when needed, I was able to clarify the question. Nevertheless, some respondents put a question mark next to the question. This implies that the question was not clear, which might have resulted in a measurement error.

Furthermore, she suggests a potential definition problem:

Still, it is possible that the question was clear to most respondents. If that was the case there must be another cause for the absence of a PC in almost all cases. Often, PAI were professionally guided, that is: people were getting paid for motivating and guiding participants. It might be that the enthusiasm of a person or a team, whether getting paid for it or not, is sufficient. This would imply that the definition of a PC needs to be changed. I used the definition: 'someone who voluntarily devotes time and energy to the success of the implemented intervention'. If the reasoning above is true, the new definition would not include the word 'voluntarily' anymore.

The researcher also made conclusions about the other six hypotheses (H1, H3, H5, H6, H7, H8). Inspection of the data table in Figure 5.2 reveals that all successful cases have also PRA (Perceived relative advantage), KI (Knowledge intervention), FR (Financial resources), and C (Costs). Consequently, the corresponding four hypotheses H1, H3, H5, and H8 are supported (not falsified). Because at least one case is in the upper left corner for IC (Individual commitment), and T (Triability), corresponding to the deterministic view on necessity, the researcher considered these conditions not necessary for success, and the corresponding hypotheses H6 and H7 were rejected (falsified).

EXAMPLE OF NCA WITH THE SCATTER PLOT APPROACH

The second example is about Corporate Social Responsibility (CSR). Companies can have two reasons to engage in CSR initiatives: to make a positive contribution to society or to support their own strategic goals from the perspective that CSR is just business. Skarmeas and Leonidou (2013) performed a large N study (504 customers) about factors that contribute to customer scepticism about a company's CSR initiative. Skarmeas and Leonidou (2013) and Skarmeas et al. (2014) performed three types of data analysis with this dataset: multiple regression, structural equation modelling, and fuzzy-set QCA. The first two analysis approaches intend to identify contributing factors *on average*, and the third data analysis approach intends to identify *combinations of factors* that are sufficient for the outcome. I will use their dataset to evaluate whether *single factors* are *necessary* for customer scepticism about the company's motives for CSR. This example can also be used to show how NCA can complement regression analysis and QCA (see the supplementary material on the NCA website (www.erim.nl/nca)). I first present how I formulate the necessary conditions (Stage 1), then how Skarmeas and Leonidou (2013) collected the data (Stage 2), and finally how I analysed the data with the six steps of NCA's scatter plot approach by using the NCA software (Stage 3).

Stage 1: Formulation of necessary condition hypothesis

The goal of this research is to avoid customer scepticism about the motives of an organisation's CSR initiative, which can be formulated with the general research question 'Which factors contribute to customer scepticism about CSR initiatives?'. This research question is practically relevant, because factors may be influenced by the organisation, and the outcome is undesirable. Originally, Skarmeas and Leonidou (2013) used *average effect* logic to find the contributing factors. I will use necessity logic. The specific research question is 'Which factors *are necessary* for customer scepticism about CSR initiatives?'. The necessity logic would be more implicit when one of the constraining descriptions of Box 2.1 is used, e.g. 'Which factors *limit* customer scepticism about CSR initiatives?'. For answering their original research question the researchers first explored the literature about potential contributing factors to scepticism in general. They selected four factors that were linked on average to CSR scepticism: egoistic-driven motives, strategic-driven motives, stakeholder-driven motives and value-driven motives. In a later study, Skarmeas et al. (2014) suggest that each contributing factor could theoretically also be a necessary condition for CSR scepticisms. Hence, four necessary condition hypotheses can be formulated:

- H1: A high level of egoistic-driven motives is necessary for a high level of customer scepticism.
- H2: A low level of value-driven motives is necessary for a high level of customer scepticism.
- H3: A high level of strategic-driven motives is necessary a high level of customer scepticism.
- H4: A high level of stakeholder-driven motives is necessary for a high level of customer scepticism.

Notice that in H2 a low level of X is necessary for a high level of Y whereas in the other hypotheses high levels of X and necessary for high levels of Y.

Stage 2: Collect data

The research strategy was a large N observational study. The researchers selected customers of companies with CSR initiatives using an online platform. This initial convenience sample consisted of 520 cases. For each case the four independent variables and the dependent variables were measured with a standardised questionnaire. The respondents were asked to recall and specify a grocery retailer that they had recently visited, and to complete the questionnaire about this retailer. Sixteen respondents were eliminated for reasons of measurement validity and incomplete data. Hence, the final dataset contained data from 504 cases. A selection of ten cases from the dataset is shown in Figure 5.4. For all variables the minimum and maximum scores are 1 and 7, respectively. Because the scores of the most variables are constructed by taking the average from four items with a seven-point rating scale, the variable is discrete with 25 possible levels (from 4/4 to 28/4).

	A	B	C	D	E	F
1	Case	Egoistic-driven motives	Value-driven motives	Strategy-driven motives	Stakeholder-driven motives	Scepticism
2	1	7.00	2.00	6.50	2.50	5.75
3	2	5.33	4.00	5.75	3.00	2.50
4	3	4.00	4.00	6.75	5.00	5.00
5	4	6.00	6.00	6.00	6.00	2.00
6	5	4.00	6.00	6.00	4.50	4.00
7	6	4.00	5.00	4.25	2.75	3.00
8	7	5.67	5.75	6.50	5.75	4.75
9	8	3.33	4.50	4.50	4.25	1.75
10	9	4.00	6.00	6.75	5.25	2.50
11	10	5.67	3.50	4.50	6.00	2.75

Figure 5.4 Dataset with a selection of 10 cases from 504 cases with the scores of the four potential necessary conditions and the outcome (Scepticim).

(After Skarmeas et al., 2014.)

Stage 3: Analyse data

Step 1: Make the scatter plot

The NCA software in R is used to make the four scatter plots for the four hypotheses (Figure 5.5).

Step 2: Identify the empty space

The scatter plots of Figure 5.5 show that according to the expectation the empty spaces for egoistic-driven motives (H1) and strategy-driven motives (H3) are in the upper left corner, and for value-driven motives (H2) in the upper right corner. For these hypotheses the analysis can continue with Step 3.

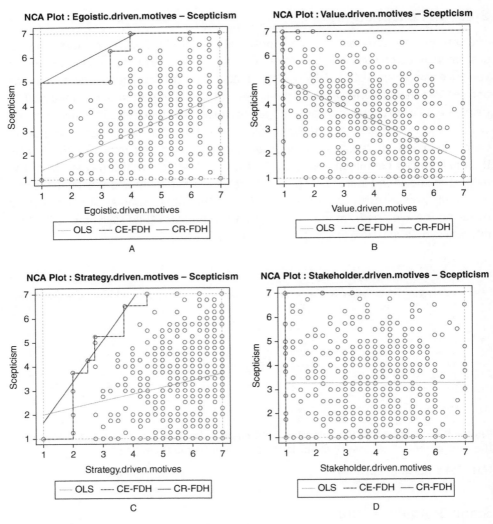

Figure 5.5   The four scatter plots of the CSR example

(data from Skarmeas et al., 2014**)**

For stakeholder-driven motives (H4) an empty space was expected in the upper left corner, but this corner has several cases. Hence, it is possible to have high level of Scepticism with a low level of Stakeholder-driven motives. For this hypothesis the analysis continues with Step 6.

Step 3: Draw the ceiling line

Before drawing the ceiling line in the scatter plot for value-driven motives (Figure 5.5B), I move the empty space from the upper right corner to the upper left corner by flipping the X-axis, using `flip.x = TRUE` in the `nca_analysis` instruction.

The highest X score is now on the left and the lowest X-score is on the right (Figure 5.6). The reason is that the hypothesis reads that a *low level* of X is necessary for a high level of Y, and the NCA software evaluates the NCA parameters assuming an empty space in the upper left corner. By defining a new X* as the absence of X, the empty space will be in the upper left corner.

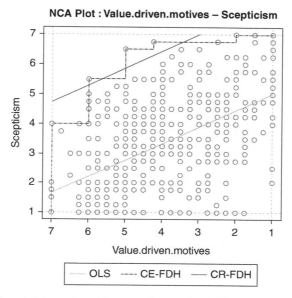

NCA Plot : Value.driven.motives – Scepticism

Figure 5.6 Scatter plot for value-driven motives using a flipped X-axis ensuring that the expected empty space is in the upper left corner

Hence, the three scatter plots in which a ceiling line will be drawn are Figure 5.5A, Figure 5.5C and Figure 5.6. In these scatter plots the two default ceiling lines CE-FDH and CR-FDH are drawn. Because of the irregular shape of the ceiling observations for the conditions egoistic-driven motives and value-driven motives, the CE-FDH ceiling line seems to be a better choice than the CR-FDH ceiling line. I report only results for the CE-FDH ceiling line.

Step 4: Quantify the NCA parameters

The NCA parameters ceiling zone, scope, effect size, and c-accuracy are shown in Table 5.1. The c-accuracy of the CE-FDH ceiling line is 100% by definition.

Step 5: Evaluate the NCA parameters

The c-accuracy is maximum. I set a threshold value of $d = 0.1$ for evaluating the *substantive* significance of the effect size. According to the general benchmark, an effect

Table 5.1 NCA parameters for the example with the scatter plot approach

	Egoistic-driven motives	Value-driven motives	Strategic-driven motives
ceiling zone (C)	5.162	5.438	10.438
Scope (S)	36	36	36
effect size (d)	0.143	0.151	0.29
c-accuracy	100%	100%	100%
p value	0.079	0	0.004

size below 0.1 can be considered as a small effect. Table 5.1 shows that the observed effect sizes ranges from 0.14–0.29, which is above 0.1, hence these effect sizes can be considered as meaningful. I set a threshold of $p = 0.05$ for evaluating the *statistical* significance of the effect size. Table 5.1 shows the results of the statistical test with 10,000 permutations. It turns out that the p value of the effect size for egoistic-driven motives is 0.079, which is above the threshold p value of 0.05. Hence, the observed effect size of egoistic-driven motives could be due to random chance of unrelated variables. The p value for value-driven motives is virtually 0 and for strategy-driven motives 0.004, which are both well below the threshold p value of 0.05. Hence, the observed effect sizes for value-driven motives and strategy-driven motives are likely not caused by random chance of unrelated variables.

Step 6: Formulate the conclusion

Table 5.2 summarises the findings regarding the hypotheses' theoretical support, substantive significance in terms of effect size of at least 0.1, and statistical significance in terms of p value less than or equal to 0.05. These are three minimum criteria for supporting the hypothesis.

Table 5.2 Summary of the findings for the scatter plot example

	Theoretical Support?	$d \geq 0.1$?	$p \leq 0.05$?
Egoistic-driven motives	Yes	Yes	No
Values-driven motives	Yes	Yes	Yes
Strategy-driven motives	Yes	Yes	Yes
Stakeholder-driven motives	Yes	No	No

The results show that all four hypotheses are theoretically supported. The effect size for three hypotheses is at least 0.1, except for the hypothesis for Stakeholder-driven motives. The p value for two hypotheses is less than or equal to 0.05. Because all three criteria must be met for supporting the hypothesis, only Value-driven motives and strategy-driven motives could be considered as necessary conditions. Their substantive significance (d ≥ 0.1) and the statistical significance ($p ≤ 0.05$) are strong enough to not falsify the necessary condition hypothesis. Hypothesis H2, formulated in kind, is 'The absence of value-driven motives is necessary for the presence of customer scepticism', and hypothesis H3, formulated in kind, is 'Strategic-driven motives is necessary for customer scepticism'. The bottleneck table (Figure 5.7) shows what level of X is required for a given level of Y, and allows hypothesis formulations in degree. The bottleneck table gives insight about which levels of both the necessary conditions are required for a certain level of Y. The bottleneck table for the CE-FDH ceiling line for the two necessary conditions is shown in Figure 5.7.

```
> model<-nca_analysis(data,c(2,3),5, ceilings= "ce_fdh",flip.x = c(T,F), bott
leneck.x = "actual", bottleneck.y = "actual", step.size = 1)
> nca_output(model, summaries = F, bottlenecks = T)
-------------------------------------------------------------------------
Bottleneck CE-FDH (cutoff = 0)
Y Scepticism                   (actual)
1 Value.driven.motives         (actual)
2 Strategy.driven.motives (actual)
-------------------------------------------------------------------------
Y        1       2
1       NN      NN
2       NN      2.000
3       NN      2.000
4       NN      2.500
5       6.000   2.750
6       5.000   3.750
7       2.000   4.500
```

Figure 5.7 Output from the NCA software in R for the CSR example with the bottleneck table. NN means 'not necessary'.

The bottleneck table is produced with actual values of the variables. Furthermore, the outcome has a step size of 1 ranging from 1 to 7. The table shows that for outcome level Y = 1 Value-driven moties and Stategy-driven motives are not necessary (NN). For outcome levels 2–3 only Strategy-driven motives are necessary with a required level of 2. This required level of the condition increases for higher outcome levels. For outcome level 5 or more also Value-driven motives is necessary. For Scepticism level 5 it is necessary to have level 6 of Value-driven motives and level 2.75 of Strategy-driven motives. For Scepticism level 6 it is necessary to have level 5 of Value-driven motives and level 3.75 of Strategy-driven motives, etc. Because the outcome is undesirable (Scepticism) each of the necessary conditions can prevent a high level of Scepticism. Value-driven motives can prevent level 5 scepticism when its score is above 6, and Strategy-driven motives can prevent this level of scepticism when its score is below 2.75. The condition Strategy-driven motives can also prevent lower levels of Scepticism. Any level of Scepticism from 2 to 7 can be prevented by Strategy-driven motives if its value is below 2.

EXAMPLE OF NCA IN OPERATIONS MANAGEMENT RESEARCH (KNOL ET AL., 2018)

Knol et al. (2018) presented a study on 'Implementing lean practices in manufacturing SME's: testing "critical success factors" using Necessary Condition Analysis'. Lean manufacturing is a popular manufacturing approach that focuses on meeting customer demands with minimum manufacturing time. The authors reviewed the literature on lean manufacturing, total quality management and just in time management to identify 12 critical success factors for lean practices, and then tested the necessity of those factors.

Contribution

In the introduction the authors discuss the meaning of 'critical success factors' in lean manufacturing and consider them as necessary but not sufficient conditions. They refer to the literature to justify this necessity interpretation, e.g. by referring to the statement that critical success factors in lean manufacturing are 'areas of managerial planning and action that must be practised to achieve effective quality management in a business unit' (2018: 3955). They also refer to Herzberg's (1968) notion of 'hygiene factors' which do not guarantee job satisfaction, but do need to be in place to prevent dissatisfaction. They contrast necessity logic with the current notion about the relative 'importance' of factors for success. Hence, the authors aim to provide a theoretical contribution by considering critical success factors not as 'important' factors but as 'necessary but not sufficient' factors. They test this theoretical idea by using NCA: 'So the general assumption for manufacturing SMEs is that success factors need to be present before lean practices can be implemented' (p. 3956).

Hypothesis

The authors formulate necessary condition hypotheses based on an evaluation of the literature about important lean manufacturing factors that contribute to performance on average. They find 12 critical success factors that they consider as necessary for a successful implementation of lean manufacturing. Hence, implicitly they formulate 12 necessary condition hypotheses. The 12 potential necessary conditions (Xs) for successful implementation of lean manufacturing are 'top management support', 'shared improvement vision', 'good communication', 'leadership', 'people focus', 'learning focus', 'sufficient resources', 'improvement training', 'performance measurement system', 'supplier link', 'customer link' and 'support congruence'. The focal unit of the hypotheses is manufacturing SME, with apparently no geographical or other limit for the theoretical domain.

Methods

Data

The authors do not discuss their *research strategy*, but it is implied to be a large N observational study. They use convenience *sampling* by selecting 33 manufacturing SMEs from the network of the authors' research group. For the *measurement* the authors used multiple informants from each company (average six, always including the production manager) to measure the 12 conditions and the outcome. The informants rated each condition on a nine-point scale that was explained to the informant by the researcher. The score for the condition was the mean score of all informants in the company. Further, the informants rated the outcome 'extent of implementation' by answering 41 questions using five-point scales. The mean score of all answers was used as the score of the extent of implementation of lean practices.

Data analysis

The authors justify the selection of the two *ceiling lines* Ceiling Envelopment – Free Disposal Hull (CE-FDH) and Ceiling Regression – Free Disposal Hull (CR-FDH) by stating that the X and Y variables could both be interpreted as having a discrete number of levels, which justifies CE-FDH, as well as being nearly continuous, which justifies CR-FDH. The authors state that 'almost every scatter plot contains a ceiling zone, no matter how small, in its upper-left corner' (Knol et al., 2017: p. 3964), and they implicitly use an *effect size threshold* > 0 to accept the necessity hypothesis: 'Visual inspection of all figures indeed showed an empty space in the upper-left corner of each figure. These empty spaces indicated that all 12 success factors were necessary for implementing lean practices' (p. 3961). The authors did not statistically test the effect size, because such a test was not available at the time they performed their study.

Results

The authors report the results by presenting all 12 *scatter plots*, *effect sizes* and *ceiling accuracies* for the two ceiling techniques. The authors base their substantive evaluation of the effect size on the general benchmark. All observed effect sizes were considered 'moderate' to 'large'. The authors conclude that the 12 hypotheses are supported because no effect size is zero. They also perform a *bottleneck table* analysis with the 12 conditions that are necessary. The bottleneck table can give insights on the combined necessity effects of several conditions to enable a given level of the outcome. For example, the authors report that 'This bottleneck table suggests that the only success factors critical for some implementation of lean practices [the authors refer to the level of the outcome being about 20%] are good communication, a learning focus, an improvement structure (sufficient resources, improvement training and a performance measurement system) and support congruence, and that the most critical factors for more advanced lean practitioners [the authors refer to the required level of the condition being more than 80%] are a shared improvement vision, leadership and a supplier link' (p. 3968). One note here is that the wording's 'most critical factors' may be somewhat confusing because all factors that are necessary are equally critical: they all can individually block the outcome.

The conclusion that all 12 conditions are necessary may be premature because the effect sizes may be the result of random chance of unrelated variables. Since the statistical randomness test was not available at the time of this study, the authors provided me with their data so I could perform the test. The results of the NCA approximate permutation are shown in Table 5.3.

Table 5.3 Statistical significance test for the effect sizes reported in Knol et al., 2018

Hypothesis	Effect size (original article)		p value (this book)	
	CE-FDH	CR-FDH	CE-FDH	CR-FDH
Top mgt. support is necessary for Lean production	0.25	0.21	**0.140**	**0.128**
Shared impr. vision is necessary for Lean production	0.29	0.30	0.015	0.003
Good comm. is necessary for Lean production	0.29	0.28	0.001	0.001
Leadership is necessary for Lean production	0.22	0.20	**0.057**	**0.056**
People focus is necessary for Lean production	0.20	0.16	0.035	0.093
Learning focus is necessary for Lean production	0.30	0.27	0.001	0.003
Sufficient resources is necessary for Lean production	0.28	0.26	0.018	0.020
Impr. training is necessary for Lean production	0.39	0.34	0.000	0.000
Performance mgt. is necessary for Lean production	0.29	0.23	0.001	0.021
Supplier link is necessary for Lean production	0.35	0.30	0.003	0.011
Customer link is necessary for Lean production	0.16	0.10	**0.340**	**0.486**
Support congruence is necessary for Lean prod.	0.36	0.30	0.000	0.002

The test shows that for most hypotheses the p values are below 0.05, hence the data do not appear to be compatible with the null hypothesis that states that the observed effect is due to random chance of unrelated variables. The data may thus support these hypotheses. However, the effect sizes of two factors in particular, namely Top management support and Customer link, appear to be compatible with the null hypothesis, and therefore may not represent necessity. Top management support may be important on average for successful lean production implementation, but may not be necessary for it. Customer link refers to collaboration with customers about production improvements, and the statistical test found no support that this is necessary for successful implementation. This may be due to unreliable measurement of this concept because informants may have confused it with customer focus, which is an important but different concept (Knol, personal communication January 30, 2018).

This article is an example of a straightforward NCA analysis with a new and relatively small dataset. It is the first application of NCA in research on the implementation of lean manufacturing.

EXAMPLE OF NCA IN ENTREPRENEURSHIP RESEARCH (ARENIUS ET AL., 2017)

In their article 'No particular action needed? A Necessary Condition Analysis of gestation activities and firm emergence', Arenius et al. (2017) report a study on 'gestation activities', which are entrepreneurial actions for establishing a new firm. The article is relatively short and focuses on necessity logic and NCA. The authors tested 25 necessary conditions hypotheses, and did the test six times with different existing datasets. One reason that the article is illustrative is that nearly all necessary conditions were rejected and yet an important contribution could be made.

Contribution

In the introduction the authors describe the current belief that 'entrepreneurship requires action' and refer to studies that have identified the specific actions that new entrepreneurs commonly take during the start-up process. Examples of these actions are doing initial market research, setting up a team, and getting funding. These activities are considered important for becoming a successful company, but are they also necessary? The authors point to the fact that the existing research focuses on factors or combinations of factors that produce the outcome by stating 'Despite conventional wisdom and broad scholarly agreement that gestation activities do matter, empirically speaking, the jury is still out on the relative importance of each individual activity, as well as how complex configurations of gestation activities shape entrepreneurial outcomes' (p. 87). Hence, the authors implicitly refer to current regression studies when writing about the 'relative importance of each individual activity', and to current Qualitative Comparative Analysis (QCA) studies when writing about 'complex configurations of gestation activities'. Arenius et al. conclude their description of the current state of the art by saying that 'In sum, prior research seem to have reached an empirical dead-end in trying to identify gestation activities as sufficient conditions for firm emergence, that is - we still don't know what complex combinations of single conditions are more likely to explain firm emergence' (p. 87).

The authors propose to shift the consensus of sufficiency thinking, thus outcome producing thinking, towards necessity thinking by making the following *theoretical contribution*: 'In the current article, we suggest ... a shift in the logic of examination from one of sufficiency to that of necessity' (p. 87). Specifically they formulate their contributions as follows:

> We therefore aim to offer a number of important contributions to the literature by exploring whether (1) certain gestation activities; (2) a certain number of gestation activities; and (3) certain categories of gestation activities, are necessary for firm emergence to occur. For our empirical tests, we apply a new methodological technique termed 'Necessary Condition Analysis' (NCA) [...] on a recently harmonized dataset of nascent entrepreneurs across four countries [...] NCA is particularly useful in situations where several predictors (e.g., gestation activities) contribute to the desired outcome (e.g., firm emergence) but none of the predictors is sufficient. In such instances, NCA can identify both critical predictors and critical levels of these predictors that must be present to achieve the desired outcome. (p. 88)

The main contribution of this article is a theoretical contribution by using the necessity logic. There is also a methodological contribution by applying NCA. The authors mention that their study can contribute to practice but do not specify this contribution.

Hypothesis

The authors formulate several hypotheses. The first set of hypotheses deal with 18 gestation activities that were part of the overall dataset (see below). They suggest that each of these activities are necessary for firm success, hence 18 necessary condition hypotheses were formulated. Second, the authors formulate the hypothesis that the number of activities is necessary for success. Third, they group gestation activities into six categories selected from the literature: public presence, operations, infrastructure, planning, funding, and complexity. They state that successful start-up firms need each specific category of activities, resulting in another six necessary condition hypotheses. The focal unit of the hypotheses is 'firm'. The theoretical domain is not specified; it might be that this theory is considered to apply to any start-up firm in the world.

Methods

Data

The authors did not collect the data themselves. They used existing datasets to test the hypotheses. They obtained five datasets that they call 'samples' from different countries (Australia, Sweden, China, and two datasets from the USA). They also combined the datasets into one 'overall' dataset of 3537 active nascent entrepreneurs. Hence, the hypotheses are tested six times: five times with separate datasets and one time with the total dataset. The authors emphasise that the data are longitudinal with large N; the implied *research strategy* is a large N observational study. Regarding *sampling* they consider the country datasets as representative for startups in the respective countries. It is unknown which population is represented by the overall dataset. For the *measurement* of the independent variables, which are the potential necessary conditions, they refer to the literature in which the dataset is explained without giving details about measurement scores, e.g. about levels – dichotomous, discrete, or continuous. Questionnaires were used to collect the data. From the scatter plots it can be observed that profit is dichotomous, namely 'yes' or 'no' profit after 24 months and that the number of gestation activities is discrete with 2–18 levels.

Data analysis

The authors use the two default *ceiling lines* Ceiling Envelopment – Free Disposal Hull (CE-FDH) and Ceiling Regression – Free Disposal Hull (CR-FDH) without further explanation. Note that the hypothesis about the number of activities and profit could be best analysed with CE-FDH because the outcome is dichotomous. The effect size calculated with CR-FDH is then half as large as the effect size calculated with CE-FDH. For evaluating the effect size the authors use *effect size thresholds* corresponding to the general benchmark, and consider a necessary condition being absent if the effect size is below 0.1. A *statistical test* for the effect size was not performed because such a test was not available at the time of their study.

Results

Given the limited space, the authors present *scatter plots* for one hypothesis only: the relationship between number of gestation activities and profit. For this hypothesis they show the scatter plot for each dataset including the total dataset, hence six scatter plots. The *effect sizes* are not reported for this hypothesis, but it can be observed that five scatter plots have no empty space in the upper left corner, thus the effect size is zero. For the one exception the effect size is not given, but it can be observed that the CE-FDH effect size is $1/16 = 0.06$, hence below the 0.1 threshold that was selected by the authors. Nevertheless, the authors concluded that 'Overall our findings suggest that some level of activity is required for firm emergence within the chosen period of time' (p. 89). They based their conclusion on five plots showing that with two or more activities profit is possible, and one plot showing that with three or more activities the outcome is possible.

For the 18 hypotheses about the necessity relation between gestation activities and profit no scatter plots are shown, but the effect sizes are given. All effect sizes are 0. Also for the six hypotheses about the necessity relation between categories of gestation activities and profit no scatter plots are provided, but it is explained that none of the categories was necessary. The authors also provide results with different operationalisations of success and different subsamples and find similar results, showing the robustness of their finding that most hypotheses should be rejected. Note that the authors implicitly use a deterministic view on necessity (see Chapter 'Philosophical Assumptions and Logic of NCA', section 'Deterministic and probabilistic views on necessity' p. 17), such that one case in the upper left corner can reject the hypothesis. The authors do not present a *bottleneck table* because this makes no sense when the effect size is zero.

Having rejections of hypotheses is a valuable result and can provide important insights. The authors conclude that 'not performing one of the eighteen gestation activities does not prevent firm emergence operationalized as initial profit at 24 months' (p. 89), and thus 'no particular gestation activities are necessary' (p. 90). They continue by saying that 'This is very surprising given the assumption that gestation activities are universally important across organizations and industries ... Our unexpected results provide reasons ... for future theoretical and empirical work to reconsider long-standing assumptions about the role of gestation activities in firm emergence'.

This article is an example of a straightforward NCA analysis with existing datasets. The article is relatively short. Despite the fact that nearly all hypotheses were rejected, it provides important new theoretical insights, which can give new direction to future research.

EXAMPLE OF NCA IN STRATEGY RESEARCH (THO, 2018)

Tho (2018) presents a study on 'Firm capabilities and performance: a Necessary Condition Analysis'. In the Resource Based View (RBV) of the firm, a firm must use a collection of resources and capabilities to achieve competitive advantage. The article focuses on two such capabilities: marketing capability and innovativeness capability. The author tests whether these capabilities are necessary for firm performance.

Contribution

By referring to the literature the author explains the importance of firm capabilities, defined as a bundle of knowledge and skills as an *enabler* of the firm's performance. He mentions literature that focuses on the average effect of firm capabilities on performance, and subsequently cites Eisenhardt and Martin (2000: 1106) to highlight another way of looking at the relationship between firm capabilities and performance: 'capabilities are necessary, but not sufficient, conditions for competitive advantage' (Tho, 2018: 323). The author states that 'to the best of the author's knowledge, however, the question of what level of each capability serving as a necessary condition for a wanted level of performance has been largely ignored in the literature' (p. 323). He therefore proposes NCA 'to investigate the levels of necessity of two key firm capabilities ... for firm performance' (p. 323). With 'level of necessity' of a capability for performance, the author meant (personal communication 21 December 2018) the 'level of capability that is necessary for a certain level of performance' as the necessity itself has no degree. Hence, the theoretical contribution of this article is to use necessity logic to describe the relationship between capabilities and performance, and the methodological contribution is to apply NCA for the first time in this field of research.

Hypothesis

In the section 'Theory and hypotheses', the author continues the literature review and explains why the two selected capabilities can be considered as necessary conditions. He subdivides the marketing capability into four separate capabilities and implicitly formulates five necessary condition hypotheses in degree by stating, 'Formally, this study proposes that marketing capability, comprising responsiveness to customers, responsiveness to competitors, responsiveness to the macro environment, and business relationship quality, and innovativeness capability are necessary conditions, but at different levels, for firm performance' (p. 324).

Methods

Data

The author does not discuss his *research strategy*, but it is implied to be a large N observational study. He apparently used convenience *sampling* by selecting a variety of 311 manufacturing and service firms in Ho Chi Minh City, Vietnam. For the *measurement* a senior manager of the firm was used as informant who was interviewed face to face. A questionnaire was employed using multi-item, seven-point Likert scales. Scores of the six variables were captured by taking the mean of the item scores of the variables.

Data analysis

The author uses the two default *ceiling lines* Ceiling Envelopment - Free Disposal Hull (CE-FDH) and Ceiling Regression - Free Disposal Hull (CR-FDH) without further explanation. For evaluating the effect size the author does not mention an *effect size threshold* but apparently considers a necessary condition being present when the effect size is greater than zero. A *statistical test* for the effect size was not performed because such a test was not available at the time of their study.

Although the article's main contribution is the use of necessity logic and the application of NCA, apparently for comparison, the article also analyses the data by using a standard multiple regression analysis for estimating the capabilities' average effects on performance. The regression analysis includes not only the five capabilities but also control variables. Note that control variables are needed in regression analysis because not including them may give biased results. Such 'omitted variable bias' may occur when variables that correlate with both the independent variable and the dependent variable are not included as control variables in the regression analysis. However, control variables are not needed for NCA as the necessary condition operates in isolation from the rest of the causal structure, and the results are not affected by adding or omitting other variables.

Results

The author presents the five *scatter plots* to evaluate the necessity relationship between the capabilities and performance. The *effect sizes* are not reported for all capabilities. All five scatter plots have the expected empty space in the upper left corner, thus the effect size is non-zero. The author only presents the highest and second highest effect size. The highest effect sizes were for responsiveness to customers being 0.158 and 0.136 for CE-FDH and CR-FDH, respectively. The author presents the bottleneck table and discusses this table and its meaning for practice extensively: 'Firms ... should specify the target level of performance and then identify the [necessary] level .... of each capability for their performance target' (p. 330). He states, for example, that

> 'the findings indicate that, in order to reach 60 percent level of performance, business relationship quality and innovativeness capability are not necessary conditions for firm performance but other capabilities are required to reach a ... [target performance] level (responsiveness to customers: 26.2 percent; responsiveness to competitor: 22.6 percent; responsiveness to the macro environment: 17.5 percent). When increasing the level of performance (e.g., 80 percent level), all of these capabilities are necessary conditions for firm performance but at different levels (responsiveness to customers: 33.3 percent; responsiveness to competitor: 22.6 percent; responsiveness to the macro environment: 17.5 percent; business relationship quality: 25.0 percent; and, innovativeness capability: 20.0 percent)' (p. 330).

This article is an example of a straightforward NCA analysis that makes a theoretical, methodological and practical contribution.

EXAMPLE OF NCA IN INNOVATION RESEARCH (VAN DER VALK ET AL., 2016)

Van der Valk et al.'s (2016) article entitled 'When are contracts and trust necessary for innovation in buyer-supplier relations? A Necessary Condition Analysis' studied how buyer firms can stimulate supplier firms regarding supplier-led innovation of outsourced processes, products and services. Contracts and trust are considered two important factors that contribute to successful supplier-led innovation. Contracts relates to the level of detail of the contract between the buyer and supplier firm. Trust has two dimensions. Goodwill trust relates to the intention to fulfil an agreed role in the collaboration, and competence trust relates to the ability to fulfil that role. The authors suggest that contract detail, goodwill trust, and competence trust may be necessary conditions for high innovation performance.

Contribution

The article intends to make three contributions. The first contribution is methodological by applying necessity logic and NCA. The article is published in a special issue about new methodology in purchasing and supply management research. A full section in the article deals with 'The logic of necessary conditions' that includes the subsections 'The NCA technique' and 'Necessity thinking and NCA versus sufficiency thinking and Regression'. The article contrasts necessity logic with sufficiency logic. The authors argue that current interpretations of regression-based research focus on sufficiency: predictors are sufficient causes for increasing (producing) the outcome. They introduce NCA as 'an additional logic and data analysis tool for a more fine-grained understanding of purchasing and supply management phenomena' (p. 267). The article's second contribution is theoretical. The literature mentions two theoretical views about the combined effect of contracts and trust for successful performance. In the 'substitute' view contracts *or* trust contribute to the outcome, and in the 'complement' view contract *and* trust contribute to the outcome. By using necessity logic the authors argue that the complement view would be supported if both contract and trust are necessary for successful collaborative innovation.

Hypothesis

In the section 'Theoretical background', the authors review governance and innovation literature regarding the role of contracts and trust for innovation performance. The literature considers contracts and trust as *contributing* factors for innovation on average, not as *necessary* factors, although the literature also hints at the necessity of contracts and trust. The authors state that it is worthwhile to explicitly consider them also as necessary conditions for innovation: 'Contracts and trust in relation to innovation have to date not been viewed or analyzed in terms of necessity. Therefore, NCA is applied to existing data on contracts, trust and (supplier-led) innovation' (p. 268). The authors only implicitly formulate the three necessary condition hypotheses, i.e. that contractual detail, goodwill trust and competence trust are necessary for innovation in buyer-supplier relations: 'Given the exploratory nature, this article does not state or test formal hypotheses, but explores presumed relationships' (p. 269).

Methods

Data

The study uses a survey *research strategy*, hence a large N observational study. The focal unit of the implicit hypotheses is 'buyer-supplier relation'. The selected population consisted of Dutch buyer-supplier relations for maintenance services. The *sampling* of buyer-supplier relations was done via buyer members of a Dutch professional association for asset owners and maintenance service providers. The buyer selected a buyer-supplier relation by selecting a contract. All 430 buyer members were approached but only 75 members reacted, and useful information was available from 48 members. Hence, the resulting sample of buyer-supplier relations is a non-probability sample. For the *measurement* the buyer member was the informant about the buyer-supplier relation that they selected. A questionnaire was employed using multi-item, five- or seven-point Likert scales. Scores of the four variables were captured by taking the mean of the item scores of the variables.

Data analysis

The authors used the two default *ceiling lines* Ceiling Envelopment - Free Disposal Hull (CE-FDH) and Ceiling Regression - Free Disposal Hull (CR-FDH) without further explanation. For evaluating the effect size the authors used the general benchmark *effect size thresholds*. The authors did not perform a *statistical test* for the effect size because such a test was not available at the time of their study.

Results

The authors present the *scatter plots* to evaluate the necessity relationship between contractual detail, goodwill trust and competence trust, and innovation. The authors provide detailed information about several NCA parameters including *effect size, accuracy, ceiling zone*, and *scope*. Their *substantive evaluation of the effect size* is based on the general benchmark and shows that all three factors had a medium to large effect size. The authors concluded that the three conditions are necessary for innovation performance. Recently, the data were reanalysed for performing a *statistical evaluation of effect size* (Dul et al., forthcoming). This test showed that the *p* values are low ($p < 0.05$), suggesting that the results may not be due to random chance of unrelated variables. The authors present the *bottleneck table* and discuss this table and its meaning for practice extensively. Based on the bottleneck table the authors formulate three classes of innovation: low innovation up to 52% innovation that is achieved by half of the buyer-supplier relationships where no condition is necessary for innovation; high innovation from 79-100% is achieved by only 10% buyer-supplier relationships where high levels of the conditions are necessary to achieve this level of innovation; and medium innovation where only small to medium levels of the conditions are necessary. The authors suggest that the results may provide two practical contributions: (1) avoid failure of innovation and (2) avoid waste of resources for innovation. For avoiding failure the authors state that 'this article provides insight into which conditions need to be met when seeking supplier-led innovation in service outsourcing relationships, as well as in the required levels of these conditions' (p. 274). For avoiding waste, the authors state that 'this article provides insights into the extent to which organizations make efficient use of their resources. In case of lower than desired innovation performance, this article directs managerial attention to those conditions that actually should be put in place or strengthened in order to achieve the desired, higher level of innovation. In contrast, organizations that have over-invested in certain conditions, may redirect their efforts to more important matters, which are the bottlenecks, i.e., the conditions that are below the necessary threshold levels for achieving the desired outcome' (p. 274).

This article is an example of making a theoretical, methodological and also practical contribution, even with a limited dataset.

SUMMARY

This chapter presented six illustrative examples of the application of NCA in different business and management fields. The examples showed that with NCA new theoretical, practical and methodological insights can be obtained that can contribute to the existing body of knowledge in these fields. The examples also show how necessary condition hypotheses can be developed (see also Appendix 1) and how the NCA methodology for testing these hypotheses and the test results can be reported (see also Appendix 3). The variety of specialised topics in the examples that are described here, as well as in other published examples in a variety of research fields (for an up-to-date overview see the NCA website at www.erim.eur.nl/necessary-condition-analysis/publications/) shows that NCA can be applied to virtually any business and management field and subfield and beyond. When you apply NCA to your area of expertise, you may be one of the first researchers to do so. By applying NCA you can help to shape how it is best applied and reported.

6

STRENGTHS AND WEAKNESSES

INTRODUCTION

This book shows how to conduct NCA. In Chapter 2 I presented the philosophical assumptions and logic of NCA, in Chapter 3 I laid out the basic components of NCA (hypotheses, data, and data analysis), and in Chapter 4 I explained how NCA's data analysis should be performed. I distinguished between NCA's contingency table approach with qualitative data analysis using visual inspection and an NCA scatter plot approach with quantitative data analysis using the NCA software with R. Chapter 5 illustrated how NCA is applied in published research in various business and management fields.

Any research method has its strengths and weaknesses, NCA as well. It is important to know these, because only then may a defensible choice of the research method be made. Knowledge about a method's weaknesses also allows a proper

Table 6.1 Strength and weaknesses of NCA

Strengths	Weaknesses
Newness	Newness
Necessity logic	Non-dominant logic
Parsimonious theory	Theory is not about presence of the outcome
Simple data collection	Possibly sensitive to outliers
Straightforward data analysis	Unresolved on what is the 'best' ceiling line
Broadly applicable	Inferential statistics not fully developed
Practically relevant	
Opportunity for interesting publications	

handling of those weaknesses and a proper reporting of remaining weaknesses (see also Appendix 3). In this chapter I discuss some strengths and weaknesses of NCA. These are summarised in Table 6.1.

STRENGTHS

Newness

NCA is a relatively new method in comparison to established methods. The method uses a new logic and a new data analysis approach that gives a fresh look at existing knowledge and data. In research NCA can be used to enhance existing theories or create new theories. In practice, the results of NCA can be used for defining new ways of designing, managing or controlling factors to influence an outcome. Consequently, findings with NCA can potentially have a great impact on research and in practice. An editor of a top journal in management demonstrated this as follows: 'From my perspective, [this NCA article] is the most interesting paper I have handled at this journal, insofar as it really represents a new way to think about data analyses'. However, newness has also a downside, which I discuss under weaknesses and illustrate with a hesitant reaction from another editor.

Necessity logic

NCA's necessity logic is intuitive. The first paragraph of this book mentioned several everyday examples of necessity logic that everyone can easily pick up. Furthermore, necessity logic is everywhere around us, and thus necessary condition statements can be found in any research area. The fact that necessity logic is intuitive and widely existing means that one can quickly understand why you have started a research project with NCA.

Parsimonious theory

The goal of a causal theory is to predict an outcome when the causes are known. Necessity theories are able to almost perfectly predict the absence of an outcome with a simple theory. Necessary theories are parsimonious theories: only one or a few factors are usually included. Each single factor can almost perfectly predict *the absence* of a certain level of the outcome when a certain level of the factor is absent. Then the factor is a bottleneck or a constraint for the outcome. When the necessity factor is present at the right level it *enables* the outcome. When it is absent at the right level it *constrains* the outcome. Hence, for having the outcome it is critical, essential, necessary, to have this factor in place: 'must have' rather than 'nice to have'. Absent necessary causes are very strong predictors of the absence of the outcome. When limited time is available for data collection and data analysis, for example in a Master's thesis research project, a study with a parsimonious theory can make an important contribution by stating that one or a few factors may or may not be a necessary condition.

Simple data collection

For empirically developing and testing hypotheses, data are needed, hence you must obtain the scores of all variables that are part of the hypotheses: the causes and the outcome. Because necessity theories are parsimonious, few variables are needed, such that the data collection is relatively simple. It is also possible to use existing datasets from yourself, of other researchers or that are available in the public domain. Such datasets may contain scores of the variables of your necessary condition hypothesis. The dataset may have been used before for other purposes, for example for testing hypotheses that are based on additive logic and average effects with regression analysis. A new contribution is possible when NCA is applied to the same dataset.

Straightforward data analysis

NCA's data analysis is straightforward both with the contingency table approach and the scatter plot approach. NCA is basically a bivariate XY analysis. The result of such analysis does not depend on the presence or absence of other variables. Also control variables are not needed because there is no risk of 'omitted variable bias'. The quantitative analysis can be done with the NCA software in R. Even if you do not know R yet, you can do the analysis rapidly.

Basically, both NCA analyses consist of identifying empty corners without cases in the graphical representation of X and Y in the contingency table or in the scatter plot. With NCA's effect size, i.e. the relative emptiness of the empty space, a necessary condition hypothesis can be evaluated regarding its substantive and statistical significance. A statistical analysis of the effect size does not require advanced statistical knowledge. Furthermore, NCA's statistical significance test does not require assumptions about the distribution of the data or other major assumptions. The only assumption is that the data are a probability sample from the population, which is a common requirement for a statistical test.

Broadly applicable

NCA is a generic empirical research methodology that can be applied broadly. NCA can be applied to any topic in the technical, medical and social sciences if a potential necessary condition can be formulated and theoretically justified. NCA is applicable in a Master's research project, a PhD research project, or any other research project. In such a project, NCA might be the main methodology, but it could also complement other methodologies for additional insights, e.g. complementing a regression-based study or complementing a QCA study (see the supplementary material on the NCA website) (www.erim.nl/nca) NCA can be used with any type of research philosophy. It has mainly been used within a positivist framework, but might also be applied within an interpretivist or other philosophical framework. Most NCA studies are observational studies using a small N case study research strategy or a large N survey strategy. However, NCA can also be applied in experimental research designs. Further, it can be used with any type of case selection or sampling strategy such as purposive sampling, probability sampling and convenience sampling, with any type of dataset with qualitative scores or quantitative scores, and with two different data analysis approaches: qualitative visual inspection or quantitative statistical analysis. Indeed, NCA is a versatile methodology.

Practically relevant

The practical usefulness of an NCA study is clear cut. If a necessary condition is identified the condition must be put and kept in place in practice to enable the outcome to exist. The absence of the condition cannot be compensated by other factors. If the condition is absent at the necessary level, it makes no sense to work on other factors that contribute to the outcome to increase the outcome. Hence, NCA can help to avoid failure and a waste of resources. Examples of such findings can be found in the NCA studies by Tho (2018), and Van der Valk et al. (2016).

Opportunity for interesting publications

With NCA, a novel theoretical, practical and methodological contribution to the literature is possible because a new logic and a new methodology can give new insights into a certain field. Publications with novelty, including theses and journal articles, are appreciated in science. You are expected to come up with new understandings and a new logic and a tool like NCA can help you reach that goal. Because NCA is new, no or only a few other researchers in your field may have used the method, so you might be the first researcher in your area who applies the method. Specifically, when a necessary condition is identified, the new insight might be that a factor that was previously considered 'just' important, may now be labelled as 'crucial' or 'critical'. Thus, the factor cannot be left out. It must be included in a theoretical model that intends to explain the outcome, and in the set of practical guidelines to produce the outcome. Also when no necessary condition is identified, the factor that was previously considered as crucial for an outcome is actually not crucial, and can be replaced by other factors.

An example of such a finding is an NCA study by Arenius et al. (2017). Furthermore, with an NCA publication, be it a thesis or an article, you can help to shape 'best practice' for applying the method and the best way to publish with the method.

WEAKNESSES

Newness

Although newness is a strength of NCA, it is also certainly a weakness. Many researchers are not familiar with the method, in particular when compared to mainstream logics, analyses and methods such as sufficiency logic, average effect analyses and regression methods. When people are uninformed about NCA they may be unsure about how the method works and about the quality of the method. An editor of a top journal in management demonstrated this hesitation as follows: 'the fact that NCA is so new and requires validation and perhaps even endorsement by top journals, limits your contribution rather than enhances it'.

NCA's newness triggers many questions about NCA and how it is applied, even questions that are not asked anymore for established methods, or questions that are not about NCA itself, but rather are universal questions that apply to any empirical research methodology. Examples of such questions are 'Can NCA prove causality?', or 'Is NCA sensitive to bad sampling?' with obvious answers, i.e. 'No' and 'Yes' respectively. Furthermore, in comparison to established methods, only a limited number of examples of NCA applications exist and standards of good practice and good reporting have not yet crystallised.

Although NCA's newness will change over time, you may be confronted with the drawbacks of applying a new method. The best way to handle this is to be knowledgeable about NCA, and to acknowledge its strengths and weaknesses. You might refer to successful applications of NCA. You may share experiences with other NCA researchers on how to handle newness. And last but not least you may enjoy being an innovator.

Non-dominant logic

Most people understand and use the word 'cause' implicitly in the meaning of sufficient cause, not as necessary cause. Studies about the psychology of causal reasoning show that people interpret data patterns in terms of sufficiency, not in terms of necessity, even if both interpretations are equally valid (Mandel and Lehman, 1998). Furthermore, when we look at a scatter plot we focus on the data points, not on the empty spaces. In our statistical courses we are taught to analyse the full space, not the empty space. We want to know how to bake a cake, not how we can fail to bake a cake. A weakness of NCA is that it uses a non-dominant necessity logic. When the focus is on another logic it needs effort and explicit thinking to capture this logic and see the value of it. Often when discussing necessity and necessity reasoning, suddenly the reasoning returns to sufficiency reasoning without notice, and hence to what we are used to thinking about. Similarly, when peers such as supervisors and reviewers comment on an NCA study, often their argumentation is based on sufficiency logic, not on necessity logic. The only way to handle this weakness of NCA is to be repeatedly explicit about NCA's underlying different logic in publications and discussions.

Theory is not about the presence of the outcome

A fundamental limitation of a necessity theory is that it only predicts the absence of the outcome, not the presence of the outcome. NCA focuses on necessity of single factors that enable or block the outcome, not on how to produce the outcome. This is a serious limitation because ultimately we are interested in how the outcome can be produced. Even though this is very difficult in the social sciences - I even called it a 'mission impossible' in Chapter 3 'Basic Components of NCA', section 'Theory' - all efforts in causal research are focused on this goal, and NCA's contribution to predict how the outcome *cannot* be achieved might be considered as a limited contribution to that goal. Although in certain fields the set of identified necessary conditions might be jointly sufficient for the outcome (e.g. Van Rhee and Dul, 2018), in other research fields this might not apply. It is also possible that no single necessary condition exists because all the factors can compensate for each other. In that case NCA does not provide additional insights other than the conclusion that necessary conditions do not exist, and no single factor can block the outcome.

This weakness can be handled by acknowledging that NCA does not predict the presence of the outcome and referring to the majority of other data analysis approaches that are equipped for predicting the presence of the outcome, at least for predicting the *average* outcome.

Possibly sensitive to outliers

Like other data analysis methods, NCA results can be sensitive to outlier cases. But what is different from other data analysis methods, in particular average effect methods, is that NCA may be more sensitive to outliers near the ceiling line. One reason for this is that the ceiling line primarily uses the upper cases from all available cases. If one such case is an outlier, the effect of the outlier on the ceiling line and the necessity effect size may be large. This contrasts average effect models where all cases are used to estimate the central tendency, such that the results may be less sensitive to an outlier.

To handle this weakness of NCA, it is important to prevent outliers that are due to errors. Outliers due to measurement error can be prevented by performing good measurement. Outliers due to sample error can be prevented by good case selec-tion and sampling. Furthermore, cases that are near the ceiling line or cases that determine the scope (cases with minimum and maximum values of X and Y) can be checked for being outliers. Outliers that are caused by sample error or unrepairable measurement error should be deleted. Giving attention to cases around the ceiling can also be beneficial for another reason. When the outcome is something that is desired and the condition is something that takes effort, cases around the ceiling may be labelled as 'best cases' in terms of efficiency: these cases were able to pro-duce the highest desired outcome for a given effort, or similarly, had least effort for a reaching a given outcome. These cases can be used for benchmarking purposes.

Unresolved on what is the 'best' ceiling line

In NCA's data analysis with discrete or continuous variables you can choose several ceiling lines as the borderline between the space without cases and the space with cases. Although two default lines are proposed based on the data or theoretical con-siderations, namely Ceiling Envelopment – Free Disposal Hull (CE-FDH) and Ceiling Regression – Free Disposal Hull (CR-FDH), no strict guideline is available about when to use which line. Currently, the use of the CE-FDH ceiling line, which is a step func-tion, can be justified in two situations. In the first situation the variables are discrete with a relatively small number of levels. In the second situation the border between the empty and full space is irregular. Also the CR-FDH ceiling line, which is a straight line, can be justified in two situations: in the first the variables are continuous or discrete with a relatively large number of levels, and in the second theory suggests that the ceiling line is straight. Further work is needed on the criteria for the 'best' line, in particular what is the 'best' line for statistical inference under given assump-tions by applying criteria such as 'unbiasedness' and 'efficiency'. Such research on the 'best' ceiling line, e.g. with simulations, may result in new definitions of ceiling lines. This weakness can be handled by selecting the ceiling line on the basis of 'best available' justification. Also, it is possible to perform the analysis with the two default ceiling lines when both lines could be selected for different reasons, and perform a robustness test by comparing the results. This approach has been employed by several researchers (e.g. Van der Valk et al., 2016; Luther et al., 2017; Knol et al., 2018).

Inferential statistics not fully developed

In the current phase of development of NCA its inferential statistics are not yet fully developed. NCA currently provides *descriptive statistics* of the data such as effect size, and *c*-accuracy. It also provides *inferential statistics* in terms of a statistical significance test (p value) for the effect size based on the approximate permutation test in order to check if the observed effect size could be caused by two unrelated variables. Although these statistical tools will serve most needs, more statistical development would be desirable for a better statistical understanding of the method. For example, the NCA statistical toolbox could be extended with the estimation of confidence intervals, which needs to be developed because standard analytical or bootstrapping approaches do not work for NCA, or the toolbox could be extended with more advanced methods like Bayesian statistics. Although this weakness of NCA does not immediately affect the analysis, it can be handled by acknowledging that confidence levels, Bayesian statistics and other advance statistical tools are not yet available for NCA.

CONCLUSION

Having read this book, and with this list of NCA's strengths and weaknesses, you will better understand the characteristics of NCA and its possibilities and limitations. I hope that you are now able to apply the method in your research project, just as many others have done before you. An updated overview of published NCA research can be found on the NCA website (www.erim.nl/nca). This website also has a special section about this book, where you can find supplementary materials. You can also leave comments on the book, such that I can improve it when I come to update it. If you need further information, or want to express ideas, you could connect with the NCA community via the NCA website or at conferences.

I hope that opening this book was a good choice.

GLOSSARY

Absolute inefficiency   The total area of the scope where the necessary condition does not constrain the outcome and the outcome is not constrained by the necessary condition. Also see *Condition inefficiency, Outcome inefficiency, Relative inefficiency.*

Accuracy   See *Ceiling accuracy, p value accuracy.*

Additive logic   A causal logic in which causes can compentate for each other. Also see *Necessity logic, Sufficiency logic.*

Analytical generalisation   The statement that the results from a specific study also apply to a wider part of the theoretical domain based on theoretical analysis and reasoning. Also see *Statistical generalisation.*

Approximate permutation test   A statistical test that produces an estimate of the *p* value by randomly selecting a large sample from all possible values of the effect size under rearrangements of the labels of the cases in order to approximate the distribution of the effect size under the null hypothesis. Also see *Permutation test.*

Binary logic   Two-valued logic where statements can only be true or false. Also see *Causal logic, Conditional logic.*

Bivariate analysis   A statistical analysis with two variables. Also see *Multiple bivariate analysis.*

Boolean logic   See *Binary logic.*

Bottleneck table   A tabular representation of the ceiling line(s) showing which values of the condition(s) is/are necessary for a given value of the outcome Y. Also see *Ceiling line.*

c-accuracy   See *Ceiling accuracy.*

Case   An instance of a focal unit. Also see *Focal unit*.

Case selection   The selection of one or a small number of cases from a set of cases for inclusion in a small N study. Also see *Sampling, Small N study*.

Case study   A research strategy in which one or a small number of cases is selected for a small N observational study. Also see *Experiment, Survey*.

Causal logic   The logic in which statements are causal relations. Also see *Binary logic, Conditional logic*.

Causal relation   A relation between two variable characteristics X and Y of a focal unit in which a value of X (or its change) permits, or results in, a value of Y (or in its change). Also see *Cause*.

Cause   A variable characteristic X of a focal unit of which the value (or its change) permits, or results in, a value (or its change) of another variable characteristic Y. Also see *Necessary condition, Sufficient condition*.

CE-FDH   A step function ceiling line based on the free disposal hull. Also see *CR-FDH*.

Ceiling accuracy   The extent to which cases are on or below the ceiling line expressed as a percentage of the total number of cases.

Ceiling Envelopment - Free Disposal Hull See *CE-FDH*.

Ceiling line   The borderline in an XY scatter plot or XY contingency table between the space (virtually) without cases and the space with cases. See *CE-FDH, CR-FDH* .

Ceiling Regression - Free Disposal Hull See *CR-FDH*.

Ceiling zone   The (virtually) empty space above the ceiling line.

Concept   The variable aspect of a focal unit of a proposition. Also see *Dependent concept, Independent concept, Variable*.

Conceptual model   A visual representation of a proposition or hypothesis in which the concepts or variables are presented by rectangles and the relation between them by an arrow. The arrow originates in the independent concept/variable and points to the dependent concept/variable.

Condition   A variable characteristic X of a focal unit of which the value (or its change) permits, or results in, a value (or its change) of another variable characteristic Y (which is called the 'outcome'). Also see *Independent concept, Independent variable, Necessary condition, Outcome, Sufficient condition*.

Conditional logic   If-then statements that can only be true or false. Also see *Binary logic*.

Condition inefficiency   The area of the scope where the condition does not constrain the outcome. Also see *Absolute inefficiency, Outcome inefficiency, Relative inefficiency*.

Contingency table   A matrix representation of the relation between condition and outcome with the number of cases shown in the cells. Also see *Scatter plot*.

Continuous necessary condition   A necessary condition in which the condition and the outcome can have infinite numbers of levels (values). Also see *Dichotomous necessary condition, Discrete necessary condition*.

Control variable   A variable that is added in regression-based data analyses for improving the prediction of the outcome and avoiding a biased estimation of regression coefficients. Also see *Dependent variable, Independent variable*.

Convenience sample   A non-probability sample in which the instances are selected for the convenience of the researcher. Also see *Probability sample, Random sample*.

CR-FDH   A straight ceiling line based on a trend line through the upper left peers of the free disposal hull. Also see *CE-FDH*.

d See *Effect size*.

Data   Recordings of evidence generated in the process of data collection. Also see *Measurement*.

Data analysis   The interpretation of scores obtained in a study in order to generate the result of the study. Also see *Qualitative data analysis, Quantitative data analysis*.

Data collection   The process of identifying and selecting one or more objects of measurement, extracting evidence of the value of the relevant variable characteristics from these objects, and recording this evidence. Also see *Object of measurement*.

Dataset   A collection of scores obtained from data collection.

Dependent concept   A variable characteristic Y of a focal unit of a proposition of which the value (or its change) is the result of, or is permitted by, a value (or its change) of another variable characteristic X (which is called the 'independent concept'). Also see *Independent concept*.

Dependent variable   A variable characteristic Y of a focal unit of a hypothesis of which the value (or its change) is the result of, or is permitted by, a value (or its change) of another variable characteristic X (which is called the 'independent concept'). Also see *Independent variable*.

Deterministic view   A position taken by the researcher that a condition can only be called a 'necessary condition' for an outcome when there are not exceptions. Also see *Probabilistic view*.

Dichotomous necessary condition   A necessary condition in which the condition and the outcome can have only two levels (values). Also see *Continuous necessary condition*, *Discrete necessary condition*.

Discrete necessary condition   A necessary condition in which the condition and the outcome can have finite numbers of levels (values). Also see *Continuous necessary condition*, *Dichotomous necessary condition*.

Domain   See *Theoretical domain*.

Effect size   The magnitude of the constraint that a necessary condition poses on the outcome expressed as the size of the ceiling zone relative to the size of the scope.

Effect size threshold   The *d* value selected by the researcher for evaluating the necessary condition hypothesis. Also see *Statistical significance threshold*.

Empirical scope   The area of a contingency table or a scatter plot defined by the empirically observed minimum and maximum values of the condition and the outcome. Also see *Theoretical scope*.

Expected pattern   A score or a combination of scores that is predicted by a hypothesis. Also see *Observed pattern*, *Pattern matching*.

Experiment   A research strategy in which the independent variable is manipulated and the dependent variable is measured. Also see *Case study*, *Survey*.

Falsification   The view that theories and hypotheses cannot be proven true, but can only be proven false.

Fit   The effect size of a selected ceiling line as a percentage of the effect size of the CE-FDH ceiling line.

Focal unit   The stable characteristic of a theory, proposition or hypothesis. Examples are 'employee', 'team', 'company', 'country'. Also see *Theoretical domain*.

Generalisation   The statement that the research results from a specific study also apply to a wider part of the theoretical domain. Also see *Analytical generalisation*, *Statistical generalisation*.

Hypothesis   A theoretical statement about the relationship between variables. Also see *Necessary condition hypothesis*, *Proposition*.

Independent concept   A variable characteristic X of the focal unit of a proposition, of which the value (or its change) permits, or results in, a value (or its change) of another variable characteristic Y (which is called the 'dependent concept'). Also see *Dependent concept*.

Independent variable   A variable characteristic X of the focal unit of a hypothesis, of which the value (or its change) permits, or results in, a value (or its change) of another variable characteristic Y (which is called the 'dependent variable'). Also see *Dependent variable*.

Influential case   A case that has a large influence on the necessity effect size when removed. Also see *Outlier*.

Informant   A person who is the object of measurement for a variable and who is knowledgable about that variable and informs the researcher about it. Also see *Subject*.

Instance of a focal unit   One occurrence of the focal unit.

Large N study   A study with a large number of cases. N stands for the number of cases. Also see *Small N study*.

Likert scale   A rating scale in the format of a limited number of points that can represent a person's response. Also see *Informant*, *Subject*.

Logic   See *Additive logic*, *Binary logic*, *Causal logic*, *Conditional logic*, *Necessity logic*, *Sufficiency logic*.

Measurement   The process in which scores are generated for data analysis. Also see *Data*, *Measurement reliability*, *Measurement validity*.

Measurement reliability   The degree of precision of a score. Also see *Measurement validity*.

Measurement validity   The extent to which procedures of data collection and of scoring can be considered to meaningfully capture the ideas contained in the concept of which the value is measured. Also see *Measurement reliability*.

Mediator   A concept or variable that links the independent and the dependent concept or variable in a proposition or hypothesis.

Moderator   A concept or variable that qualifies the relation between the independent and the dependent concepts or variables in a proposition or hypothesis.

Multiple bivariate analysis   A series of bivariate analyses.

Multiple regression   A technique for modelling and analysing the relationship between several independent variables and an dependent variable to understand how a dependent variable changes on average when the independent variables change. Also see *OLS regression*.

NCA   See *Necessary Condition Analysis*.

NCA parameters   A set of quantities to evaluate a necessary condition. See *Absolute inefficiency*, *Ceiling accuracy*, *Ceiling line*, *Ceiling zone*, *Condition inefficiency*, *Effect size*, *Fit*, *Outcome inefficiency*, *Relative inefficiency*, *Scope*.

Necessary cause   See *Necessary condition*.

Necessary condition   A cause that must exist in order for the outcome to exist. Also see *Sufficient condition*.

Necessary Condition Analysis (NCA)   An approach and technique for modelling and analysing the necessity relations between concepts.

Necessary condition hypothesis   A theoretical statement about the necessity relationship between variables.

Necessary condition in degree   A necessary condition that is quantitative formulated as 'level X_c is necessary for level Y_c'. Also see *Necessary condition in kind*.

Necessary condition in kind   A necessary condition that is qualitatively formulated as 'X is necessary for Y'. Also see *Necessary condition in degree*.

Necessity logic   A causal logic in which the cause is a necessary condition. Also see *Sufficiency logic*.

Necessity relation   A causal relationship in which the cause is a necessary condition. Also see *Sufficiency relation*.

Object of measurement   An object that must be observed in order to extract evidence of the value of a variable (data).

Observational study   A research strategy in which variables in the real-life context are not manipulated by the researcher. Also see *Case study*, *Survey*.

Observed pattern   The score or the combination of scores obtained in a study. In data analysis, an observed pattern is compared ('matched') with an expected pattern. Also see *Expected pattern*, *Pattern matching*.

OLS regression   A technique for modelling and analysing the relationship between one or more independent variables and an dependent variable to understand how a dependent variable changes on average when the independent variables change, based on the Ordinary Least Squares estimation technique where the squared vertical distances between the cases and the regression line are minimised. See *Multiple regression*.

Omitted variable bias   The estimation error that is made when a variable is omitted from a conceptual model that is analysed statistically.

Outcome   The variable characteristic Y of a focal unit of which the value (or its change) is the result of, or is permitted by, a value (or its change) of another variable characteristic X (which is called the 'condition'). Also see *Condition*, *Dependent concept*, *Dependent variable*.

Outcome inefficiency   The area of the scope where the outcome is not constrained by the condition. Also see *Absolute inefficiency*, *Condition inefficiency*, *Relative inefficiency*.

Outlier   An outlier is a point (case) in a scatter plot or contingency table that is considered to be 'far away' from the other points (cases). Also see *Influential case*.

p-accuracy   See *p value accuracy*.

Pattern   See *Expected pattern*, *Observed pattern*.

Pattern matching   Comparing two or more patterns in order to determine whether patterns match (i.e. that they are the same) or do not match (i.e. that they differ). Pattern matching in data analysis is comparing an observed pattern with an expected pattern.

Peer   A case that is used to draw the ceiling line.

Permutation test   A statistical test that produces an exact *p* value by obtaining the distribution of the effect size under the null hypothesis by calculating all possible values of the effect size under rearrangements of the labels of the cases. Also see *Approximate permutation test*.

Probabilistic view   A position taken by the researcher that a condition can also be called a 'necessary condition' for an outcome when there are a few exceptions.

Population   The set of instances of a focal unit defined by one or a small number of criteria.

Probability sample   A sample in which each instance of a sampling frame has a known non-zero probability of being selected into the sample. Also see *Convenience sample*, *Random sample*.

Proposition   A theoretical statement about the relationship between concepts. Also see *Hypothesis*.

p value   The probability that the effect size is greater than or equal to the observed effect size when the null hypothesis that the variables are unrelated is true.

p value accuracy   The estimated difference between the exact *p* value of the effect size and the estimated *p* value of the effect size. Also see *Approximate permutation test*, *Permutation test*.

QCA   See *Qualitative Comparative Analysis*.

Qualitative Comparative Analysis (QCA)   An approach and technique for modelling and analysing the relationship between concepts and combinations of concepts by using set theory and binary logic.

Qualitative data   Scores expressed in words or letters. Also see *Quantitative data*.

Qualitative data analysis   Identifying and evaluating a pattern in the scores obtained in a study by visual inspection. Also see *Pattern matching*, *Quantitative data analysis*, *Visual inspection*.

Quantitative data   Scores expressed in numbers. Also see *Qualitative data.*

Quantitative data analysis   Generating and evaluating the output of statistical procedures applied to the scores obtained in a study. Also see *Pattern matching, Qualitative data analysis.*

Random sample   A probability sample in which each instance of the sampling frame has the same probability of being selected into the sample. Also see *Convenience sample, Probability sample.*

Rating   A method in which a person assigns a value to an object. Also see *Informant, Subject.*

Regression   see *Multiple regression, OLS regression.*

Rejection   A hypothesis is said to be rejected if the observed pattern of scores is not the same as the pattern predicted by the hypothesis. Also see *Expected pattern, Observed pattern, Pattern matching.*

Relative inefficiency   The total area of the scope where the necessary condition does not constrain the outcome and the outcome is not constrained by the necessary condition, expressed as percentage of the scope. Also see *Absolute inefficiency, Condition inefficiency, Outcome inefficiency.*

Replication   Conducting a test of a hypothesis in another instance, or in another group or population of instances of the focal unit.

Research design   See *Research strategy.*

Research strategy   A category of procedures for selecting or generating one or more instances of a focal unit .Also see *Case study, Experiment, Survey.*

Sample   A set of instances selected from a population or a theoretical domain. Also see *Convenience sample, Probability sample, Random sample.*

Sampling   The selection of instances from a population or a theoretical domain. Also see *Sample, Sampling frame.*

Sampling frame   A list of all instances of a population. Also see *Population, Probability sampling.*

Scatter plot   A graphical representation of the relation between condition and outcome on two axes with cases shown as points. Also see *Contingency table.*

Scope   The area of a contingency table or a scatter plot defined by the minimum and maximum values of the condition and the outcome. Also see *Empirical scope, Theoretical scope.*

Score   A value assigned to a variable based on data.

Significance   See *Statistical significance, Substantive significance*.

Small N study   A study with one or a small number of cases. N stands for the number of cases. Also see Large N study.

Statistical generalisation   The statement that the research results that are obtained in a sample of a population also apply to the population from which the sample is drawn. Also see *Analytical generalisation*.

Statistical significance   The meaningfulness of the effect size from a statistical perspective. Also see p value, *Substantive significance*.

Statistical significance threshold   The *p* value selected by the researcher for evaluating the necessary condition hypothesis. Also see *Effect size threshold*.

Study   A research project in which a research objective is formulated and achieved.

Subject   A person who is the object of measurement and an instance of the focal unit of the theory. Also see *Informant*.

Substantive significance   The meaningfulness of the effect size from a practical perspective. Also see *Statistical significance*.

Sufficiency logic   A causal logic in which the cause is a sufficient condition. Also see *Necessity logic*.

Sufficiency relation   A causal relationship in which the cause is a sufficient condition. Also see *Necessity relation*.

Sufficient cause   See *Sufficient condition*.

Sufficient condition   A cause that always results in an outcome. Also see *Necessary condition*.

Survey   A research strategy in which a single population of instances of the focal unit is selected for a large N observational study. Also see *Case study, Experiment*.

Test   Determining whether a hypothesis is supported or rejected in an instance or in a group or population of instances selected from the theoretical domain.

Theoretical domain   The universe of instances of a focal unit of a theory, proposition or hypothesis where the theory, proposition or hypothesis is supposed to hold.

Theoretical scope   The area of a contingency table or a scatter plot defined by the theoretically possible minimum and maximum values of the condition and the outcome. Also see *Empirical scope*.

Theory   A set of propositions regarding the relations between the variable characteristics (concepts) of a focal unit, and the description of why the relations exist.

Theory-in-use   A more or less consistent set of beliefs in practice about reality.

Variable   The variable aspect of a focal unit of a hypothesis. Also see *Concept*, *Independent variable, Dependent variable*.

Visual inspection   The procedure by which patterns are discovered or compared by looking at the scores or a graphical representation of the scores. Also see *Pattern matching, Qualitative data analysis*.

APPENDIX 1

FROM RESEARCH QUESTION TO HYPOTHESES FOR NCA

Many researchers start their research with only a general idea of their research topic. In this Appendix, I first give suggestions for how to transform a research topic into a research question, and subsequently a research question into one or more hypotheses. The suggestions apply not only to formulating necessary condition hypotheses (X is necessary for Y), but also to hypothesis formulation in general (X has an effect on Y). If your ultimate goal is to contribute not only to academic knowledge but also to practice, the outcome Y may be directly or indirectly related to something that is practically relevant, either desired or undesired. Y may be the phenomenon that has triggered your choice of the research topic such as performance, innovation, sustainability, health, success, failure, accidents, or sickness. X is something that occurs in practice and that can be directly or indirectly managed, designed or otherwise changed in practice and therefore is an actionable factor.

Formulation of hypotheses in the social sciences is more an 'art' than a methodology, but empirical *testing* of these hypotheses is hard methodology. I give four guidelines that may be useful when you move from a research topic via a research question to a hypothesis:

- Formulate your research question.
- Answer your research question.
- Formulate your hypothesis.
- Embed your hypothesis in theory.

Formulate your research question

If you have a research topic, but not yet a research question, my first guideline is to select one of the following variants of the research question:

1. Which factors influence Y?
2. What are the effects of X?
3. What is the effect of X on Y?

In the first variant you are interested in outcome Y (e.g. performance) and you would want to know the factors X that influence Y. Your research question may be 'Which factors influence Y?', without specification of the factors (Xs) that influence Y. In the second variant you are not interested in an outcome per se, but instead have an interest in a factor X that is present or happens in practice or is upcoming, and would want to know its effects. Then your research question may be 'What are the effects of X?', without specification of the effect Y. In the third variant you already have an idea about both X and Y and want to find out how these are related. Your research question may then be 'What is the effect of X on Y?'.

For developing necessary condition hypotheses, I suggest you include necessity logic in the formulation of the research question. You could refer to necessity logic by using any of the wording shown in Box 2.1. However, using the words 'necessary', 'necessity', or 'necessary condition' will give the most direct link to necessity logic. The above three variants of the research question could then be formulated in terms of necessity as follows:

1. Which factors are necessary for Y?
2. For what is X necessary?
3. Is X necessary for Y?

Answer your research question

My second guideline is to try to answer your research question. This seems odd because you want to do research to answer this question. What I mean here is that you would give a preliminary answer by making an 'educated guess'. When your research question does not yet specify the factors that cause Y (variant 1), or the effects of X (variant 2), these factors or effects can become clearer by trying to answer the question. You can guess these via logical reasoning, reading scientific and practical publications, using the internet including reading blogs, talking to practitioners, using your own personal ideas, etc. Normally it will be relatively easy to find a first speculative answer to your research question. After you have some first indications for X and Y and how they are related, you should read many scientific articles (e.g. 25–50) about your research topic. This is essential to gain a better understanding of your research question, for a good selection of the relevant factors X and effects Y, and for gaining better potential answers to your research question, and hence for making that question academically sound. Labelling your research as 'exploratory', as an excuse for not doing a thorough literature search before data collection, is undesirable. Hence, before you start the empirical part of your research in the positivist framework by testing a hypothesis, your preliminary answer to your research question will be based on the scientific literature and other sources.

When you read the literature, you will probably find publications that study the relationships between one or more potential causes (Xs) and outcomes (Ys). Most likely, these relationships have been researched as 'average effects', hence the factors contribute on average to the outcome, based on correlation analysis, regression analysis, structural equation modelling, and other average effect approaches. Such studies result in the identification of important average contributors to the outcome. These contributors may be good candidates for necessary conditions for the outcome. However, it is also possible that important average contributors are not necessary. Furthermore, it is possible that a factor that does not have a large *average effect* on the outcome is yet *necessary* for the outcome. This is possible because average effects causality is fundamentally different from necessity causality. Hence, by examining the literature and other sources, you may be able to identify *potential* necessary conditions.

It is possible to make a quick check of whether a potential necessary condition can really be necessary. You can raise the question 'Can I find or imagine cases where the outcome is present without the potential necessary condition being present?'. If the answer is 'no' there is a good reason to propose the factor as a necessary condition. If the answer is 'yes', you could raise the follow-up question 'Is this an exceptional or a-typical case and therefore should not be part of my intended theoretical domain?'. If the answer is 'no' this factor may not be a necessary condition and you might want to omit it from the list of potential necessary conditions. Basically you will have done a mental single case study to test a necessary condition. If the answer is 'yes' you can define your theoretical domain more precisely and maintain the factor as a potential necessary condition.

Formulate your hypothesis

My third guideline is to formulate your hypothesis explicitly. This is now simple because it can be based on the preliminary answer to your research question, which in all three variants of the research question is 'X is necessary for Y'. This answer equals the hypothesis. To further specify this hypothesis, the hypothesis' focal unit and theoretical domain (where it is supposed to hold) should also be specified.

The suggested format of a necessary condition hypothesis is 'X is necessary for Y'. This implies that 'the presence or high level of X is necessary for the presence or high level of Y'. It is also possible that for X or Y (or both), 'presence or a high level' must be replaced by 'absence or low level', due to the nature of the necessity relationship (see Figures 2.2 and 2.5).

Embed your hypothesis in theory

My fourth guideline is to embed your hypothesis in theory. Theory is not just a set of hypotheses. The hypothesis is about the 'what' question 'what X causes what Y?', or the 'how' question 'how X causes Y?' (by necessity). Theory also answers the underlying 'why' question 'why X causes Y?'. Theory gives the logical arguments about the nature of the causal relationship between X and Y. By reading the literature, having discussions with academic peers and practitioners, and by logical reasoning it can become clear why the presence or high level of X is essential for having the presence or high level of Y, or why the absence or low level of X blocks the presence or high level of Y. Your necessity theory can be either an enabling theory formulated by using enabling wordings, or a constraining theory formulated by using constraining wordings (see Box 2.1).

APPENDIX 2

INSTALLING R, RSTUDIO, NCA R AND IMPORTING YOUR DATASET

INSTALL R AND R STUDIO

What is R?

R is an open source programming language that is increasingly used for data analysis in different scientific fields, including the social sciences. It contains many statistical, mathematical and graphical functions that are also part of commercial statistical software such as SPSS, Stata and SAS. Additionally, R can run specific user-defined functions ('packages'). One such package is NCA. Only some basic knowledge about R, that is presented in this guide, is needed to run NCA with R.

How can you install R?

R can be installed (downloaded) on your computer from the central R-website (see below). You will need to have administration rights on your computer to install this software. The version of R that you must download depends on the platform of your computer: Windows or OS X (Mac). There is also a version for Linux.

For Windows users:

- Go to http://cran.r-project.org/bin/windows/base/
- Download 'R x.y.z for Windows', where x,y,z, is the latest version number.
- Open the downloaded file and follow the instructions (accept all defaults).

For OS X (Mac) users:

- Go to http://cran.r-project.org/bin/macosx/
- Download the correct version for your OS X.
- Open the downloaded file and follow the instructions (accept all defaults).

HOW TO INSTALL RSTUDIO

Additionally you can install RStudio, which is a user-friendly environment from which you can work with R. There are RStudio versions for Windows, OS X and Linux.

- Go to https://www.rstudio.com/products/rstudio/download/
- Select RStudio Desktop (open source license).
- Download the appropriate installer of RStudio x.y.z. for your platform (Windows, OS X, etc.).
- Follow the instructions (accept all defaults).

HOW TO START RSTUDIO

After downloading R and RStudio you can start working with R via RStudio. Go to the folder RStudio in the program files where RStudio is stored in the previous step. Open this folder, and click on the RStudio executable file. This will open the RStudio screen.

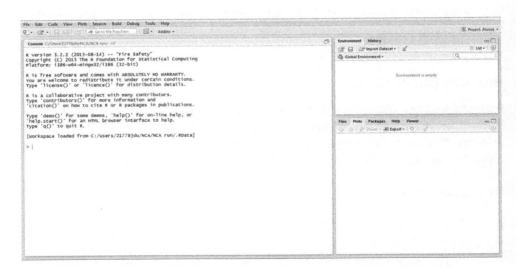

Figure A2.1 Opening of R with RStudio: the 'Console' window is on the left

RStudio opens with three windows. On the left is the window that is called 'Console'. Here you can find some basic information about R. The console displays the instructions that you give to R and numerical output if you run the instructions. Although you can type instructions after the ">" prompt and run them by giving an <enter>, I would advise you to open another window for typing instructions. In this book instructions are printed in Courier font. For certain instructions you can also use the pull down menu at the top of the RStudio page. Menu instructions are printed in Times New Roman font and successive steps are connected by an arrow '→'. A set of instructions is called a 'script'. The script window can be opened by using the pull down menu as follows: File → New File → R → Script. The window is located above the Console window. Typing instructions in the 'script window' allows you to store and replicate your script. An R script is a file with the extention '.R', for example 'Myscript.R'. You can load ('source') an existing script that is stored on your computer by using the pull down menu: File → Open File. By clicking on the 'Run' button in the script window you can successively execute each instruction line by line. You can also select several lines with instructions and run this set of instructions at once. You can edit and add instructions in the script window, and save the script by using File → Save (or using the save button), or File → Save As. RStudio displays the instructions that you run and numerical output in the console window. Graphical output is displayed in the lower right window when you click on the tab Plots. In this window the Help tab displays the manuals for the packages that are installed on your computer, including the manual for NCA. This manual provides details of all instructions and options of the NCA package. The Files tab shows the folder structure on your computer. Further information about RStudio can be found on the internet.

HOW TO SET YOUR 'WORKING DIRECTORY'

The 'working directory' is a folder on your computer where (by default) R searches your data and stores output files. You can check your current working directory by typing getwd() in the script window after the line number, followed by pushing on the Run button:

```
getwd()
```

You can change your working directory by typing:

```
setwd("...\\MyWorkingDirectory")
```

In this example the working directory is named 'MyWorkingDirectory' and the ... is the path to it. You can use any name for the working directory folder. Note that R uses "\\" in the directory tree. Alternatively you can use the forward slash "/", but not one backward slash "\".

You can also use the Files tab of the lower-right window of RStudio to select the working directory. Tick the square next to the folder that you want to select as the working directory, select More, and select Set as Working Directory. The working directory needs to be specified in R each time that you start R.

INSTALL THE NCA R PACKAGE

What is the NCA R package?

NCA is a free package for R. This package has been available since 2015 and is updated regularly: Necessary Condition Analysis. R Package. URL: http://cran.r-project.org/package=NCA.

If you have installed R and RStudio you can install the NCA R package.

How to install the NCA R package

The NCA package runs with R for Windows, OS X (Mac) and Linux. For Windows, Installation (downloading) of the NCA package for R in Windows is possible from R-version 3.0.1 for Windows. In the script window type and run:

```
install.packages("NCA")
```

Select the location nearest to you. This will install package NCA and all other R packages ('dependencies') that are used by NCA on your computer. A new version of NCA and other installed packages can be obtained by:

```
update.packages()
```


How to load the NCA R package

After the NCA package is installed (downloaded) on your computer, it must be loaded (activated) in R. NCA must be loaded each time you start R. This is done via the following instruction:

```
library(NCA)
```

After running this instruction, some basic information about NCA is displayed in the console window. If you get a warning message that the NCA package was built under a certain version of R and you have an older R version it is strongly advisable to update your R package, otherwise some NCA functions may not work properly. A simple way to update your R package is by installing the package 'installr'. It is necessary at this point to leave RStudio and update R from Rgui (which is the console window after starting R instead of starting RStudio) as follows:

```
install.packages("installr")

library(installr)

updateR()
```

During the installation process you can press 'next', 'OK', and 'Yes' on everything. Note that this process, and in particular copying of files and updating of packages, may take several minutes.

IMPORT YOUR DATASET IN R

How to prepare your data file

Your data may be stored as an Excel (.xlsx) file, as in Figure 4.1B. Rows correspond to cases, except for the first row, which can be a header with variable names. Columns correspond to variables, except for the first column, which can be row names, thus case identifiers. This is similar as is commonly used in data files, for example SPSS data files. Missing data are preferably left empty although NA (not applicable) could also be used. Numbers like 999 may be confusing.

You can save your .xlsx file as a .csv file (comma-separated values). Depending on the region and language settings of your computer, your Excel program will use decimal points or decimal commas, and the separator in the .csv file will be a comma or a semi-colon, respectively. I am presuming that you will have decimal points and comma separators. You can store your .csv file in the working directory of your R session. Other data file types than .csv are possible as well. Examples include SPSS data (sav), Stata data (dta), and SAS data (xpt).

How to load your data in R

You can load your .csv data file in R and give it the name 'data' as follows (if it contains a header in the first row and has row names in the first column):

```
data <- read.csv("mydata.csv", row.names = 1)
```

If your file uses decimal commas instead of decimal points, you could try using read.csv2 instead of read.csv. If your datafile contains a header but no row names you can load your data as follows:

```
data <- read.csv("mydata.csv")
```

and the rows will be identified on screen with number 1 to the total number of cases.
    If your dataset has no header (and no row names) you can type:

```
data <- read.csv("mydata.csv", header = FALSE)
```

and the columns will be identified on screen with a number from 1 to the total number of variables. For loading a dataset you can also use the Import Dataset tab in the upper-right window of RStudio. If your data file is an SPSS, SAS, or Stata file, I recommend you install the Haven package with `install.packages("haven")` and load it with `library(haven)`. The data file can then be loaded with `read_spss()` for .sav files, `read_sas()` for .sas7bdat and .sas7bcat files, and `read_dta()` for .dta files.

    For checking the data, the first or last six rows of the dataset can be displayed in the console window by typing the instructions 'head' or 'tail' and the data name:

```
head(data)
```

```
tail(data)
```

A summary of the data (minimum and maximum values etc.) can be obtained by typing:

```
summary(data)
```

After you have installed R and RStudio, installed and loaded the NCA package, and loaded your data, you can conduct a Necessary Condition Analysis (see Chapter 4).

APPENDIX 3

WRITING UP YOUR NCA STUDY

In this Appendix I give suggestions about how to report your NCA study. I am presuming here that NCA is your main logic and methodology and that you will base your narrative on this logic and methodology. In my guidelines I focus on the NCA-specific parts of the report. These guidelines should not be considered as strict rules. How to write up a study depends on personal preferences, and the preferences of supervisors, reviewers, editors, publishers, etc. The four core parts of any research publication are: Introduction, Methods, Results, Discussion. Each of these parts has NCA-specific elements as shown in Box A3.1, and that are also discussed below.

Box A.3.1 NCA-specific parts of reporting an NCA study

Introduction

- Contributions of introducing necessity logic in this research field
- Necessary condition hypotheses

Methods

- Data
  - o Research strategy
  - o Case selection/sampling
  - o Measurement

(Continued)

- Data analysis

  - Contingency table approach

    - Criteria for decision about hypothesis

  - Scatter plot approach

    - Specification of selected ceiling line(s)
    - Specification of effect size threshold (*d*)
    - Specification of statistical significance threshold (*p*)

Results

- Contingency table or scatter plot
- NCA parameters
- Effect size evaluation

  - Substantive significance
  - Statistical significance

- Results of hypothesis test
- Presentation of bottleneck table

Discussion

- Theoretical contributions
- Practical contributions
- Methodological contributions
- Limitations
- Future research

INTRODUCTION

In the Introduction section you can explain the contributions of your research, which can be theoretical, practical or methodological, or a combination. The *theoretical contribution* of applying NCA is that necessity causal logic is used to study the phenomenon of interest. It is likely that until now the phenomenon has only or mostly been studied from the perspective of sufficiency causality and additive logic: factors that on average contribute to produce the outcome and can compensate for each other. A common aim of existing studies is to understand the relative influence of several single factors and how together they have an effect on the outcome. The theoretical contribution of an NCA study is that the phenomenon is now studied from a new perspective: single factors that enable a certain outcome when present at the right level, or block this outcome when this level is absent. Hence, your study is about the necessity of single factors and not how this factor on average can help produce the outcome. Your justification for choosing necessity logic can be supported by examples of necessity statements in the literature that are similar to the examples in Box 2.2. The phrases 'necessary but not sufficient' or 'necessary but insufficient' are frequently used in the literature and these may hint at necessity logic. Also phrases with words like 'required', 'prerequisite', and 'critical' and other words (see Box 2.1) may hint at necessity. This suggests that necessity logic is probably around in your research field, but that related necessity theories and hypotheses have not been formulated explicitly and have not been tested. Then your contribution is that you formulate explicitly the necessary condition hypotheses and test these with NCA. Because conventional data analysis approaches focus on average effects, they cannot assess necessity. This is why your study uses NCA, which is specifically developed for necessity analysis. You can also stress that you intend to give a *practical contribution* by applying necessity logic and NCA because this can provide results that are practically useful. The single factor that is necessary must be in place at the right level in almost all cases, otherwise the outcome will not occur. You can further state that you are giving a *methodological contribution* because you are applying a new methodology to an existing field of research. It would not be unlikely that you prove to be one of the first researchers to use NCA in your field of research.

In the introduction or in a separate section on theory or hypotheses you can formulate the necessary condition hypotheses that are being tested. You can give theoretical arguments as to why you think that the hypothesis holds, illustrated with references to the literature. You can have a focus on specific conditions (Xs) and specific outcomes (Ys) and explain why you think that there is a necessity relationship between them, e.g. by building on the arguments that have been used by other researchers to justify that X has an average effect on Y. You could emphasise that you have a parsimonious model with only a few variables, and that this is possible because you study factors that are necessary but not sufficient. You are not attempting to study if the potentially necessary factors contribute also on average to the outcome. It is important to stress that the necessary condition model can be simple because the necessary condition operates isolated from the rest of the causal structure. This results in the formulation of one or more necessary condition hypotheses, preferably as a necessary condition in kind, 'X is necessary for Y', as a qualitative hypothesis is commonplace.

METHODS

In the 'Methods' section you can describe how you have used NCA. You need to provide a level of detail that will allow other researchers to replicate your analysis. In particular, you must describe the details on where the data came from and how they were analysed with NCA. Regarding data you need to show how you obtained your existing or new dataset by explaining your *research strategy*. That research strategy can be the experiment, or one of the two types of observational study: the case study, or the survey. You also describe the *case selection or the sampling* from the theoretical domain. Regarding sampling you must specify the population and select a random sample, which is preferred, or a convenience sample, which is common. Further, you will need to specify the *measurement*, including how you collected the data, e.g. with interviews, observations, questionnaires, objective data collection, and what measures and procedures were used to obtain the final scores in the dataset. These methodological parts are usually not specific for NCA, with two exceptions. First, when you have done an experiment you must explain how the necessity experiment worked, as this will not be known by most readers. The manipulation consists of taking away or reducing the necessary condition. Second, when you have used purposive sampling with cases where the outcome is present in a small N study, you must explain why such a purposive sample is possible for necessity logic, i.e. your attempt to falsify the necessary condition in cases where the outcome is present. You should describe what your criteria were for 'outcome is present' and explain why you selected the specific case(s) where the outcome is present.

The data analysis is core to the NCA methodology and you should describe in detail the methods you used for this. When you have used the *contingency table approach* with a small number of cases (e.g. < 20) and X and Y are dichotomous variables, you can explain that you rejected the hypothesis when even a single case showed up in the expected empty cell. When you have a large number of cases, for example as in the GRE example of Figure 2.3, you may want to allow a small number of exceptions in the expected empty cell, and state that the condition is 'almost always' or 'practically' necessary, hence adopting a probabilistic view on necessity. When X and Y are dichotomous variables the empty space of interest always has one size: one cell is empty and the effect size is 1. When X or Y is discrete, the effect size can vary between 0 and 1 depending on the number of empty cells and the total number of cells (see equation 1 in Chapter 4). You may then also want to base your decision about the necessary condition hypothesis on whether or not the effect size is larger than a given threshold *d*-value. A common threshold value is 0.1.

When you have used the *scatter plot approach* and the NCA software, you will first need to justify the *ceiling line(s)* that you have used. In most applications the Ceiling Envelopment – Free Disposal Hull (CE-FDH) is used for discrete data with a few levels (e.g. up to five) or when the data around the ceiling are irregular. The line Ceiling Regression – Free Disposal Hull (CR-FDH) is used for continuous or practically continuous data or when a linear ceiling line is assumed to exist in the population. When it is hard to make a choice you can use both lines and compare the results, checking the robustness of the results. Second, you will need to specify how you evaluated the substantive and statistical significance of the effect size. You will need to base your decision on *substantive significance* by using a threshold *d*-value, for example with the common threshold value is 0.1, and on *statistical significance* by using a threshold *p* value. A common significance threshold level is 0.05, but you can decide to use a more strict level (e.g. 0.01 or 0.005) to avoid false positives when this is important. For the statistical significance test you should specify the number of permutations that you have selected for estimating the *p* value. When the computation time allows this, I would recommend you do the analysis with at least 10.000 resamples in order to gain accurate *p* value estimates (*p*-accuracy).

RESULTS

In the 'Results' section you can start with reporting the XY contingency table or the XY scatter plot for each hypothesis separately. Describe whether or not you observed an empty space in the expected corner and then reflect on possible outliers. Outliers that are clearly caused by measurement error or sample error should have been deleted. However, a researcher should be reluctant to delete outliers for other reasons. Deleting outliers should always be justified and reported.

If you have observed an empty space report on the NCA parameters including effect size. You can then report on the substantive meaning of the effect size (*d*). Do you consider the size of the effect as important or not and why? You could use the general benchmark for classifying the size of an effect. This benchmark considers an effect size of $0 < d < 0.1$ as a 'small effect', of $0.1 \leq d < 0.3$ as a 'medium effect', of $0.3 \leq d < 0.5$ as a 'large effect', and of $d \geq 0.5$ as a 'very large effect'. The statistical evaluation of effect size (*p* value) can help you evaluate if it is plausible or not that the effect size was caused by a random effect of unrelated variables. You can report the *p* value in brackets after the reported effect size. After these effect size evaluations you can make a decision about the hypothesis. The results of your hypothesis test are based on a combination of substantive and statistical significance. If you want to make a binary reject/support decision you can apply the criteria for that which you have reported in the 'Methods' section, hence the hypothesis is rejected if the effect size threshold or the statistical significance threshold are not met, or both. For example, you can claim that your hypothesis is rejected by your data when the *d* value is too small (e.g. < 0.1) and the *p* value is too large (e.g. > 0.05). With a large *d* value and a small *p* value you may want to claim that your hypothesis has been supported by your data. When the observed *p* value is smaller than the selected threshold, you will have an indication that random chance does not explain the data, but instead that another explanation exists, including potentially your hypothesis. There will always be a chance that your hypothesis is actually not true because it is possible that the effect size is a result of random chance anyway, or that another phenomenon from the one described in your hypothesis explains the effect size. Similarly, when the observed *p* value is larger than the selected threshold, you may have found a random effect, although it is still possible that your hypothesis is true. You can seek to perform replication studies to gain more confidence in your conclusion.

You can formulate a necessary condition 'in degree' by presenting the bottleneck table. This allows you to report for which level of Y which level of X is necessary. With multiple necessary conditions you can specify for a given desired level of the outcome which conditions are necessary, and for which levels. You can highlight that for certain levels of the outcome none or one condition is necessary, and that for other levels of the outcome more conditions are necessary. Hence, you can also identify combinations of conditions that are necessary for given levels of outcome.

DISCUSSION

The 'Discussion' section can start with a summary of the value of the necessity logic and approach in your specific field of research and of the main results. Next you must reflect on the results and the NCA methodology that you used for achieving those results. You will need to discuss your theoretical contributions, practical contributions, methodological contributions, the limitations of the study and possibilities for future research.

The discussion about the *theoretical contributions* of the study deals with the interpretation of the results of the hypothesis test – in particular, results that are different from expectations and not caused by sampling or measurement error, thus rejections of the hypothesis, can give rise to interesting theoretical reflections, e.g. why is the condition not necessary? Is the condition only not necessary in the part of the domain from which the cases were selected, but may it still be necessary in other parts of the theoretical domain? Can the condition be compensated for by other factors? Can a higher-order condition exist that encompasses the expected necessary condition and these compensating factors? The discussion on the theoretical contributions can refer to the theoretical expectations in the 'Introduction' section where the hypotheses were formulated.

In the discussion of the *practical contributions* of the results – when future studies would confirm the conclusions – a distinction can be made between rejected hypotheses and supported hypotheses. A rejection may mean that the condition that was supposed to be necessary does not need to be in place for achieving a desired outcome. The factor may on average contribute to the outcome, but suggesting that it is a necessary condition for the outcome may be an overstatement. The absence of the factor may be compensated for by other factors. On the other hand, a supported necessary condition must be in place in virtually all cases to allow the outcome to exist. When the level of such necessary condition is too low, the desired outcome is not possible. It then makes no sense to act on other factors, e.g. contributing factors, to increase the outcome. This will not be effective unless the bottleneck – by the absence of the right level of the necessary condition – is first removed by increasing its level.

In the discussion of the *methodological contributions* of your study you can refer to the use of necessity causal logic and NCA. You will probably be one of the first in your field to use this methodology, and can refer to other fields where the method has been used successfully. You can highlight the strengths and weaknesses of the method as you have experienced it during your study. While using NCA you may also have suggestions for its improvement and on how to use it in research. Further, you could suggest research topics where the method could also be applied.

Although in much published research only some obvious limitations are discussed, a reflection on the *limitations* of your study is an important part of your research. Researchers may feel reluctant to self-criticise their research. However, all studies have their limitations and the specific limitation of your study must be made explicit for the reader. Specifying limitations signals quality rather than weakness. These limitations are not unique for NCA and deal with virtually all the methodological choices that a researcher makes when the 'ideal' is not possible. This applies to the 'data' phase particularly. When the gold standard for research strategy, which is the experiment, cannot be realised the researcher should give arguments why this was not possible and what the consequences are of selecting a case study or survey for the interpretation of the results, e.g. regarding the limited possibility for causal interpretations. The same is true for case selection/sampling when the gold standard is not possible. For example, the sample may lack representativeness because no probability sampling was obtained, or because of a considerable non-response. The consequence here is that the statistical generalisation from the sample to the population may be biased. Also many measurement approaches have limitations, and in particular measurement validity, which means that you measure what you want to measure, and measurement reliability, which means getting the same results when the measurement is repeated, may be limited. Using measurement tools that other researchers have used in previous research, e.g. questionnaire scales, is not a guarantee of good measurement, because also previously used and published tools may have validity and reliability limitations, even if this was not discussed in these publications.

The 'Discussion' section further includes suggestions for *future research*. The discussion about the theoretical contributions and the discussion on the limitations suggest what should be done in future research. The rejection of a hypothesis, which by definition is a surprising result, might trigger new hypotheses that could be tested in a follow-up study performed by other researchers. Both the rejection and the confirmation of a hypothesis should be followed by more research in the same part or other parts of the theoretical domain, hence replication studies are always desired. Weaker parts in the research methodology should trigger suggestions for how future studies could be set up. Furthermore, you may have discovered in your data potential necessity relationships that you did not anticipate and that can be theoretically justified. These could be tested in future research.

REFERENCES

Albuquerque de Sousa, J.A., Beck, T., Bergeijk, P.A.G. van and Dijk, M.A. van (2016) 'Success and failure of nascent stock markets' (working paper). Available at https://papers.ssrn.com/sol3/papers.cfm?abstract_id=2870392

Arenius, P., Engel, Y. and Klyver, K. (2017) No particular action needed? A necessary condition analysis of gestation activities and firm emergence, *Journal of Business Venturing Insights*, *8*: 87-92.

Bakker, N. (2011) 'Necessary Conditional Hypotheses Building and Occupational Safety in Dutch Warehouses', Master's thesis, Rotterdam School of Management, Erasmus University, Netherlands. Available at https://thesis.eur.nl/pub/25725/

Baruch, Y. and Holtom, B.C. (2008) Survey response rate levels and trends in organizational research, *Human Relations*, *61*(8): 1139-60.

Braumoeller, B. and Goertz, G. (2000) The methodology of necessary conditions, *American Journal of Political Science*, *44*: 844-58.

Breet, S., Jansen, J., Dul, J. and Glaser, L. (2018) 'Is Brokerage Necessary for Innovative Performance? A Necessary Condition Analysis'. Paper presented at the Sunbelt Conference, June 26-July 1, Utrecht, Netherlands.

Celo, S. and Chacar, A. (2015) International coherence and MNE performance, *Journal of International Business Studies*, *46*(5): 620-28.

DeNeve, K.M. and Cooper, H. (1998) The happy personality: a meta-analysis of 137 personality traits and subjective well-being, *Psychological Bulletin*, *124*(2): 197.

De Vries, J., Koster, R. de, Rijsdijk, S. and Roy, D. (2017) Determinants of safe and productive truck driving: empirical evidence from long-haul cargo transport, *Transportation Research Part E: Logistics and Transportation Review*, *97*(1): 113-31.

De Winne, S. and Sels, L. (2010) Interrelationships between human capital, HRM and innovation in Belgian start-ups aiming at an innovation strategy, *International Journal of Human Resource Management*, *21*(11): 1863-83.

Dion, D. (1998) Evidence and inference in the comparative case study, *Comparative Politics*, *30*: 127-45.

Dul, J. (2016a) Necessary Condition Analysis (NCA): logic and methodology of 'necessary but not sufficient' causality, *Organizational Research Methods*, *19*(1): 10-52.

Dul, J. (2016b) Identifying single necessary conditions with NCA and fsQCA. *Journal of Business Research*, *69*(4), 1516-23.

Dul, J. (2018) Necessary Condition Analysis (NCA) with R (Version 3.0.1): a quick start guide, *Organizational Research Methods* 19(1), 10-52. Available at https://ssrn.com/abstract=2624981 or http://repub.eur.nl/pub/78323/

Dul, J. and Buijs, G. (2015) NCA 1.0. Available at https://cran.r-project.org/src/contrib/Archive/NCA/

Dul, J. and Hak, T. (2008) *Case Study Methodology in Business Research*. Oxford, UK: Butterworth Heinemann.

Dul, J., Hak, T., Goertz, G. and Voss, C. (2010) Necessary condition hypotheses in operations management, *International Journal of Operations & Production Management*, *30*: 1170-90.

Dul, J., Laan, E. van der and Kuik, R. (forthcoming) A statistical significance test for Necessary Condition Analysis, *Organizational Research Methods*.

Eisenhardt, K.M. and Martin, J.A. (2000) Dynamic capabilities: what are they? *Strategic Management Journal, 21*(10-11): 1105-21.

Evanschitzky, H., Eisend, M., Calantone, R.J. and Jiang, Y. (2012) Success factors of product innovation: an updated meta-analysis, *Journal of Product Innovation Management, 29* (Supplement S1): 21-37.

Ferrari, F. (2016) 'Necessary Conditions for New Ventures' Positive Performances', Master's thesis, Rotterdam School of Management, Erasmus University, Netherlands. Available at https://thesis.eur.nl/pub/35790

Finney, S. and Corbett, M. (2007) ERP implementation: a compilation and analysis of critical success factors, *Process Management Journal*, 13(3): 329-47.

Fisher, R.A. (1925) *Statistical Methods for Research Workers*. Edinburgh, UK: Oliver and Boyd.

Fredrich, V., Bouncken, R.B. and Kraus, S. (2019) The race is on: configurations of absorptive capacity, interdependence and slack resources for interorganizational learning in coopetition alliances, *Journal of Business Research*, 101: 862-868.

Galton, F. (1886) Anthropological Miscellanea: 'Regression towards mediocrity in hereditary stature', *Journal of the Anthropological Institute of Great Britain and Ireland*, *15*: 246-63.

Gans, J. and Stern, S. (2003) *Assessing Australia's Innovative Capacity in the 21st Century*. Melbourne, Australia: Intellectual Property Research Institute of Australia, University of Melbourne.

Goertz, G. (2003) 'Necessary Condition Hypotheses: A Database', in G. Goertz and H. Starr (eds), *Necessary Conditions: Theory, Methodology, and Applications* (pp. 76-94). Oxford: Rowman & Littlefield.

Goertz, G., Hak, T. and Dul, J. (2013) Ceilings and floors: where are there no observations?, *Sociological Methods & Research*, *42*(1): 3–40.

Goertz, G. and Starr, H. (eds) (2003) *Necessary Conditions: Theory, Methodology, and Applications*. New York: Rowman & Littlefield.

Groshal, S. (2005) Bad management theories are destroying good management practices, *Academy of Management Learning and Education*, *4*(1): 75–91.

Guiking, S. (2009) 'Necessary Conditions for Maintaining Physical Activity Interventions', Master's thesis, Rotterdam School of Management, Erasmus University, Netherlands.

Guilford, J.P. (1967) *The Nature of Human Intelligence*. New York: McGraw-Hill. Available at https://thesis.eur.nl/pub/24877/

Hauff, S., Guerci, M., Dul, J. and van Rhee, H. (2017) 'Is High Performance Without High Performance Work Practices Possible? A Necessary Condition Analysis', 10th Biennial International Conference Dutch HRM Network.

Helwig, L. (2014) 'Critical Success Factors for Information System Success Within the Empty Container Positioning Process', Master's thesis, Rotterdam School of Management, Erasmus University, Netherlands. Available at https://thesis.eur.nl/pub/23359/

Herzberg, F. (1968) One more time: how do you motivate employees?, *Harvard Business Review*, January-February: 53–62.

Hill, S.A. and Birkinshaw, J. (2014) Ambidexterity and survival in corporate venture units, *Journal of Management*, *40*(7): 1899–1931.

Hofstede, G. (1980) *Culture's Consequences: International Differences in Work-related Values*. Beverly Hills, CA: Sage Publications.

Hume, D. (1777) *An Enquiry Concerning Human Understanding*. London.

Huntington, S.P. (1993) The clash of civilizations?, *Foreign Affairs*, 22–49.

Huselid, M.A. and Becker, B.E. (2010) Bridging micro and macro domains: workforce differentiation and strategic human resource management, *Journal of Management*, *37*(2): 421–28.

International Institute of Business Analysis (2009) *A Guide to the Business Analysis Body of Knowledge (BABOK Guide)*, Version 2.0, International Institute of Business Analysis.

Karwowski, M., Dul, J., Gralewski, J., Jauk, E., Jankowska, D.M., Gajda, A., Chruszczewski, M.H. and Benedek, M. (2016) Is creativity without intelligence possible? A Necessary Condition Analysis, *Intelligence*, *57*: 105–17.

Karwowski, M., Kaufman, J.C., Lebuda, I., Szumski, G. and Firkowska-Mankiewicz, A. (2017) Intelligence in childhood and creative achievements in middle-age: the necessary condition approach, *Intelligence*, *64*: 36–44.

Knol, W.H., Slomp, J., Schouteten, R.L.J. and Lauche, K. (2018) Implementing lean practices in manufacturing SMEs: testing 'critical success factors' using Necessary Condition Analysis, *International Journal of Production Research*, *56*(11): 3955–73.

Kuipers, Z. (2016) 'The Effect of Capital Structure and Corporate Governance on Stock Liquidity', Master's thesis, Rotterdam School of Management, Erasmus University, Netherlands. Available at https://thesis.eur.nl/pub/35633.

Lam, S.K., Ahearne, M. and Schillewaert, N. (2012) A multinational examination of the symbolic-instrumental framework of consumer-brand identification, *Journal of International Business Studies*, *43*(3): 306-31.

Lasrado, L.A., Vatrapu, R. and Andersen, K.N. (2016) 'A Methodological Demonstration of Set-theoretical Approach to Social Media Maturity Models using Necessary Condition Analysis'. *Proceedings of the Pacific Asia Conference on Information Systems* (PACIS).

Lewin, K. (1943) Psychology and the process of group living, *Journal of Social Psychology*, *17*: 113-32.

Luther, L., Bonfils, K.A., Firmin, R.L., Buck, K.D, Choi, J., DiMaggio, G., Popolo, R., Minor, K.S. and Lysaker, P.H. (2017) Metacognition is necessary for the emergence of motivation in schizophrenia: a Necessary Condition Analysis, *Journal of Nervous and Mental Disease*, *205* (12): 960-66.

Mandel, D.R. and Lehman, D.R. (1998) Integration of contingency information in judgements of cause, covariation, and probability, *Journal of Experimental Psychology*, *127*(3): 269-85.

Martin, J.A. and Eisenhardt, K.M. (2010) Rewiring: cross-business-unit collaborations in multibusiness organizations, *Academy of Management Journal*, *53*(2): 265-301.

Meijer, T. (2014) 'Critical Success Factors of New Product Development in the Medical Industry', Master's thesis, Rotterdam School of Management, Erasmus University, Netherlands. Available at https://thesis.eur.nl/pub/24162

Minbaeva, D., Pedersen, T., Björkman, I., Fey, C.F. and Park, H.J. (2014) MNC knowledge transfer, subsidiary absorptive capacity and HRM, *Journal of International Business Studies*, *45*(1): 38-51.

Overschie, F. (2016) 'Software-based Platform Ecosystems: Relationship between Vertical Openness and Performance', Master's thesis, Rotterdam School of Management, Erasmus University, Netherlands. Available at https://thesis.eur.nl/pub/35017

Peng, M.W. and Luo, Y. (2000) Managerial ties and firm performance in a transition economy: the nature of a micro-macro link, *Academy of Management Journal*, *43*(3): 486-501.

Pepper, A., Gore, J. and Crossman, A. (2013) Are long-term incentive plans an effective and efficient way of motivating senior executives?, *Human Resource Management Journal*, *23*(1): 36-51.

Porter, M.E. (1990) The competitive advantage of nations, *Harvard Business Review*, March-April: 73-93.

Ragin, C.C. (1987) *The Comparative Method: Moving Beyond Qualitative and Quantitative Strategies*. Los Angeles: University of California Press.

Ragin, C.C. (2000) *Fuzzy-set Social Science*. Chicago: University of Chicago Press.

Ranjan, J. and Bhatnagar, V. (2008) Critical success factors for implementing CRM using data mining, *Journal of Knowledge Management Practice*, *9*(3): 1–7.

Sarrucco, E.T.S. (2011) 'Critical Success Factors of Firms that Cooperate in Innovation', Master's thesis, Rotterdam School of Management, Erasmus University, Netherlands. Available at https://thesis.eur.nl/pub/25209

Shi, B., Wang, L., Yang, J., Zhang, M. and Xu, L. (2017) Relationship between divergent thinking and intelligence: an empirical study of the Threshold Hypothesis with Chinese children, *Frontiers in Psychology*, *8*: 254.

Skarmeas, D. and Leonidou, C.N. (2013) When consumers doubt, watch out! The role of CSR scepticism, *Journal of Business Research*, *66*(10): 1831–38.

Skarmeas, D., Leonidou, C.N. and Saridakis, C. (2014) Examining the role of CSR skepticism using fuzzy-set qualitative comparative analysis, *Journal of Business Research*, *67*(9): 1796–1805.

Smits, J. (2018) 'The Necessary Conditions for Entrepreneurial Behaviour by Middle Management', Master's thesis, Rotterdam School of Management, Erasmus University, Netherlands.

Swart, J. and Kinnie, N. (2010) Organisational learning, knowledge assets and HR practices in professional service firms, *Human Resource Management Journal*, *20*(1): 64–79.

Thieule, P. (2018) 'The Role of Organizational Factors in the Pursuit of Exploratory Innovation Across Business Units: A Necessary Condition Analysis', Master's thesis, Rotterdam School of Management, Erasmus University, Netherlands.

Tho, N.D. (2018) Firm capabilities and performance: a necessary condition analysis, *Journal of Management Development*, *37*(4): 322–32.

Treadway, D.C., Breland, J.W., Williams, L.M., Cho, J., Yang, J. and Ferris, G.R. (2013) Social influence and interpersonal power in organizations: roles of performance and political skill in two studies, *Journal of Management*, *39*(6): 1529–53.

Tulkens, H. (1993) On FDH efficiency analysis: some methodological issues and applications to retail banking, courts, and urban transit, *Journal of Productivity Analysis*, *4*(1): 183–210.

Vaisey, S. (2009) QCA 3.0: The "Ragin Revolution" continues, *Contemporary Sociology*, *38*(4): 308–12.

Van Dalen, J.W. (2014) 'Explaining Employee Satisfaction with the Headquarter-Subsidiary Relationship', Master's thesis, Rotterdam School of Management, Erasmus University, Netherlands. Available at https://thesis.eur.nl/pub/20668/

Van der Laan, G. and Dul, J. (2016) 'Corporate Social Performance: A Necessary Condition Analysis'. *Proceedings of the European Academy of Management*, Paris.

Van der Valk, W., Sumo, R., Dul, J. and Schroeder, R.G. (2016) When are contracts and trust necessary for innovation in buyer-supplier relationships? A necessary condition analysis, *Journal of Purchasing and Supply Management*, *22*(4): 266–77.

Van Rhee, H. and and Dul, J. (2018) 'Filling the Black-box of HR: Unraveling the AMO Model and Elevating It to the Organizational Level', *Academy of Management Proceedings*, 2018, 13840.

Van 't Hul, E.F. (2015) 'Customer Orientation and Business Performance: A Content Analysis of Dutch SMEs' Websites', Master's thesis, Rotterdam School of Management, Erasmus University, Netherlands. Available at https://thesis.eur.nl/pub/31804

Verheul, P.L. (2013) 'Critical Success Factors for IT Project Success'. Master's thesis, Rotterdam School of Management, Erasmus University, Netherlands. Available at https://thesis.eur.nl/pub/21360.

Verhoeve, S. (2017) 'Testing the Necessary Conditions of Technology Acceptance by Potential Organizational Users of a Mandatory IT in the Pre-implementation Phase'. Master's thesis, Rotterdam School of Management, Erasmus University, Netherlands. Available at https://thesis.eur.nl/pub/41117

Vis, B. & Dul, J. (2018) Analyzing relationships of necessity not just in kind but also in degree: Complementing fsQCA with NCA. *Sociological Methods and Research*, 47(4), 872-899.

INDEX